First World War
and Army of Occupation
War Diary
France, Belgium and Germany

41 DIVISION
122 Infantry Brigade
Hampshire Regiment
15th (Service) Battalion
2 May 1916 - 31 October 1917

WO95/2634/4

The Naval & Military Press Ltd
www.nmarchive.com
Published in association with The National Archives

Published by

The Naval & Military Press Ltd

Unit 10 Ridgewood Industrial Park,

Uckfield, East Sussex,

TN22 5QE England

Tel: +44 (0) 1825 749494

www.naval-military-press.com

www.nmarchive.com

This diary has been reprinted in facsimile from the original. Any imperfections are inevitably reproduced and the quality may fall short of modern type and cartographic standards.

© Crown Copyright
Images reproduced by permission of The National Archives, London, England, 2015.

Contents

Document type	Place/Title	Date From	Date To
Heading	WO95/2634/5		
Heading	15th Bn Hampshire Regt May 1916-Oct 1917 Mar 1918-1919 Mar		
War Diary	Havre	02/05/1916	03/05/1916
War Diary	Meteren	04/05/1916	08/05/1916
War Diary	Lacreche	09/05/1916	19/05/1916
War Diary	Ploegsteert Wood & Creslow	17/05/1916	23/05/1916
War Diary	Creslow & Ploegsteert Wood	24/05/1916	30/05/1916
War Diary	La Creche	20/05/1916	28/05/1916
War Diary	Creslow	29/05/1916	30/05/1916
War Diary	Ploegsteert Wood	31/05/1916	04/06/1916
War Diary	Creslow	05/06/1916	10/06/1916
War Diary	Ploegsteert Wood	11/06/1916	30/06/1916
War Diary	Ploegsteert Wood & Creslow	01/07/1916	03/07/1916
War Diary	Creslow & Piggeries	04/07/1916	08/07/1916
War Diary	Piggeries & Front Line	09/07/1916	15/07/1916
War Diary	Front Line & Piggeries	16/07/1916	17/07/1916
War Diary	Piggeries	18/07/1916	20/07/1916
War Diary	Piggeries & Romarin	21/07/1916	26/07/1916
War Diary	Romarin & Creslow	27/07/1916	31/07/1916
War Diary	Creslow	01/08/1917	02/08/1917
War Diary	Creslow & Ploegsteert Wood	03/07/1917	08/07/1917
War Diary	Ploegsteert Wood & Creslow	09/07/1917	14/07/1917
War Diary	Creslow La Creche	14/07/1917	15/07/1917
War Diary	La Creche Meteren	16/07/1917	16/07/1917
War Diary	Meteren Fletre	17/07/1917	17/07/1917
War Diary	Creslow	01/08/1917	02/08/1917
War Diary	Creslow & Ploegsteert Wood	03/08/1917	07/08/1917
War Diary	Ploegsteert Wood & Creslow	08/08/1917	14/08/1917
War Diary	Creslow La Creche	15/08/1917	15/08/1917
War Diary	La Creche Meteren	16/08/1917	16/08/1917
War Diary	Meteren Fletre	17/08/1917	17/08/1917
War Diary	Fletre	18/08/1917	23/08/1917
War Diary	Villers Sous Ailly	24/08/1917	31/08/1917
War Diary	Fletre	18/08/1917	23/08/1917
War Diary	Villers Sous Ailly	24/08/1917	31/08/1917
War Diary	Villers-Sous-Ailly	01/09/1917	05/09/1917
War Diary	Dernancourt	05/09/1917	11/09/1917
War Diary	Fricourt	11/09/1917	12/09/1917
War Diary	Trenches W. Of Delville Wood (Attack)	13/09/1917	15/09/1917
War Diary	York Trench (Reserve)	15/09/1917	16/09/1917
War Diary	Dernancourt	17/09/1917	30/09/1917
Miscellaneous	March Table 122nd Infantry Brigade		
War Diary	Dernancourt	01/10/1918	01/10/1918
War Diary	Mametz	02/10/1918	02/10/1918
War Diary	Somme	03/10/1918	11/10/1918
War Diary	Dernancourt	12/10/1918	17/10/1918
War Diary	Abbeville	18/10/1918	20/10/1918
War Diary	Ypres Salient	21/10/1918	31/10/1918
Heading	15th (Ser) Bn. Hants Regt. November 1916		

Type	Location	From	To
War Diary	St. Eloi	01/11/1916	03/11/1916
War Diary	Reninghelst	04/11/1916	08/11/1916
War Diary	Dickebusch	09/11/1916	15/11/1916
War Diary	Chippewa Camp Reninghelst	16/11/1916	22/11/1916
War Diary	St. Eloi	23/11/1916	27/11/1916
War Diary	Chippewa Camp Reninghelst	28/11/1916	02/12/1916
War Diary	Dickebusch And Voormezeele	03/12/1916	04/12/1916
War Diary	Voormezeele And Dickebusch	04/12/1916	08/12/1916
War Diary	Chippewa Camp Reninghelst	09/12/1916	14/12/1916
War Diary	St. Eloi	15/12/1916	21/12/1916
War Diary	Chippewa Camp Reninghelst	22/12/1916	25/12/1916
War Diary	Chippewa Camp	26/12/1916	28/12/1916
War Diary	Dickebusch & Voormezeele	29/12/1916	31/12/1916
Heading	15th (Ser.) Battn Hampshire Regt. War Diary For January 1917		
War Diary	Dickebusch & Voormezeele	01/01/1917	02/01/1917
War Diary	Chippewa Camp Reninghelst	03/01/1917	07/01/1917
War Diary	St. Eloi	08/01/1917	14/01/1917
War Diary	Chippewa Camp Reninghelst	14/01/1917	21/01/1917
War Diary	Voormezeele & Dickebusch	22/01/1917	27/01/1917
War Diary	Chippewa Camp	28/01/1917	02/02/1917
War Diary	St. Eloi	03/02/1917	09/02/1917
War Diary	Chippewa Camp	10/02/1917	16/02/1917
War Diary	St Eloi	17/02/1917	22/02/1917
War Diary	Chippewa Camp	22/02/1917	26/02/1917
War Diary	St Eloi	27/02/1917	03/03/1917
War Diary	Chippewa Camp	05/03/1917	10/03/1917
War Diary	Voormezeele & Dickebusch	11/03/1917	17/03/1917
War Diary	Chippewa Camp	18/03/1917	22/03/1917
War Diary	St Eloi	23/03/1917	30/03/1917
War Diary	Chippewa Camp	31/03/1917	31/03/1917
Miscellaneous	Officer Commanding, 15th Hampshire Regt.	01/05/1917	01/05/1917
War Diary	Chippewa Camp	01/04/1917	04/04/1917
War Diary	Dickebusch	05/04/1917	12/04/1917
War Diary	Dickebusch & Chippewa Camp	13/04/1917	13/04/1917
War Diary	Chippewa Camp	14/04/1917	17/04/1917
War Diary	St Eloi	18/04/1917	23/04/1917
War Diary	Chippewa Camp	24/04/1917	24/04/1917
War Diary	Chippewa Camp & Beauvoorde	25/04/1917	25/04/1917
War Diary	Beauvoorde	26/04/1917	27/04/1917
War Diary	Beauvoorde & Lederzeele	27/04/1917	27/04/1917
War Diary	Lederzeele To Tournehem	28/04/1917	28/04/1917
War Diary	Tournehem	29/04/1917	30/04/1917
Miscellaneous	Officer Commanding, 15th Batt. Hampshire Regt.		
War Diary	Tournehem	01/05/1917	14/05/1917
War Diary	Tournehem & Lederzeele	15/05/1917	15/05/1917
War Diary	Lederzeele & Beauvoorde	16/05/1917	16/05/1917
War Diary	Beauvoorde Chippewa Camp Micmac Camp	17/05/1917	20/05/1917
War Diary	St Eloi Sector	20/05/1917	26/05/1917
War Diary	Chippewa Camp	26/05/1917	30/05/1917
War Diary	Chippewa & Micmac Camps	28/05/1917	30/05/1917
War Diary	Chippewa Camp & St Eloi	31/05/1917	31/05/1917
Miscellaneous	Officer Commanding 15th Battn. Hampshire Regt.	30/06/1917	30/06/1917
War Diary	St Eloi Sector	01/06/1917	04/06/1917
War Diary	St Eloi Sector & Middle Camp West (M.E.B.9.S)	05/06/1917	05/06/1917
War Diary	Middle Camp West	05/06/1917	05/06/1917

War Diary	Middle Camp West & Position Of Assembly For Attack (Old French Trench)	06/06/1917	07/06/1917
War Diary	Damstrasse	07/06/1917	07/06/1917
War Diary	Obscure Support	08/06/1917	08/06/1917
War Diary	Old French Trench	09/06/1917	11/06/1917
War Diary	Old French Trench & Support Line	12/06/1917	15/06/1917
War Diary	White Chateau	16/06/1917	19/06/1917
War Diary	Bivouac Camp 28. N 5 A 9.8 Gordon Farm	20/06/1917	26/06/1917
War Diary	N 2. C. 6.4 (Millekruisse)	26/06/1917	30/06/1917
Map			
Miscellaneous	C Form. Messages And Signals.		
Miscellaneous	A Form. Messages And Signals.		
War Diary	N 2. C. 5.4 (Millekruisse)	01/07/1917	11/07/1917
War Diary	27.R. 34. A.5.9 (Schaxken)	12/07/1917	22/07/1917
War Diary	Murrumbiggee Camp	23/07/1917	23/07/1917
War Diary	Murrumbiggee Camp & P & O. Trench Bois Confluent	24/07/1917	27/07/1917
War Diary	Bois Conflunet P & O Trench	28/07/1917	30/07/1917
War Diary	Pandio Trench Bois Confluent	31/07/1917	31/07/1917
War Diary	Lock House Cellers	31/07/1917	03/08/1917
War Diary	Iron Bridge Tunnels	04/08/1917	05/08/1917
War Diary	O. 5.c.7.9	05/08/1917	10/08/1917
War Diary	Murrumbidgee Camp N. 1.a.	11/08/1917	13/08/1917
War Diary	Fletre 27/W.6 H.Q. X 2.d. 0.4	14/08/1917	19/08/1917
War Diary	Staple	20/08/1917	20/08/1917
War Diary	Acquin 27A/V. 22.a	21/08/1917	23/08/1917
War Diary	Acquin	24/08/1917	31/08/1917
Map			
Miscellaneous			
War Diary	Acquin 27A/V. 22a.	01/09/1917	13/09/1917
War Diary	Wallon Cappel 27/N. 35 E	14/09/1917	14/09/1917
War Diary	Le Roucklooshille X.2.d.1.4	15/09/1917	15/09/1917
War Diary	Ridge Wood	16/09/1917	17/09/1917
War Diary	Hedge Street Tunnels 28/1.30.b. 4.7	17/09/1917	17/09/1917
War Diary	Hedge Street Tunnels	18/09/1917	22/09/1917
War Diary	To Caestre	23/09/1917	26/09/1917
War Diary	Teteghem 19/1.22.	27/09/1917	27/09/1917
War Diary	Bray Dunes	28/09/1917	29/09/1917
War Diary	Bray Dunes 19/D. 2.c.	01/10/1917	14/10/1917
War Diary	Wiltshire Camp (Coxyde Bains) 11/X. 1.b. 5.8	15/10/1917	17/10/1917
War Diary	Wiltshire Camp 11/X. 1.b. 5.8	18/10/1917	28/10/1917
War Diary	St Pol Surmer 19/H.Z.d. 65.95	29/10/1917	31/10/1917

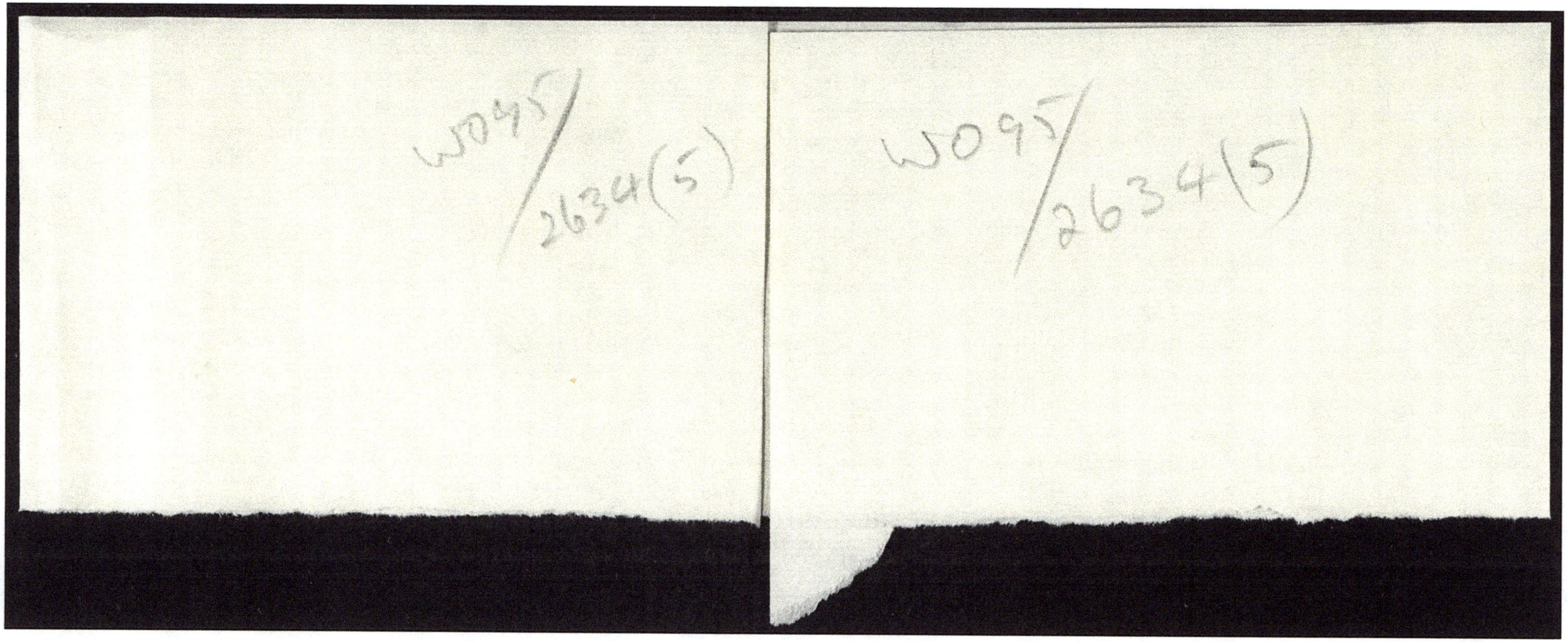

41ST DIVISION
122ND INFY BDE

15TH BN HAMPSHIRE REGT

MAY 1916 — ~~DEC 1918.~~ OCT 1917

MAR 1918 — 1919 MAR

To 29 DIV. 88 BDE

ITALY 1917 NOV — 1918 FEB

WAR DIARY
or
INTELLIGENCE SUMMARY

Army Form C. 2118

Place	Date 1916	Hour	Summary of Events and Information	Remarks and references to Appendices
HAVRE	2nd May	6 a.m.	Battalion Disembarked, marched to Rest Camp	
	3rd "		Entrained at 11.39 a.m.	
METEREN	4th "		Detrained at GODEWAERSVELDE & marched to METEREN	
	5th "		In Billets at METEREN	
	8th "		"	
LA CRÈCHE	9th "		Marched from METEREN into Billets at LA CRÈCHE area.	
	10th "		In Billets at LA CRÈCHE (12 Officers 40 NCOs proceeded for 2 days instruction in trenches being attached to 11th Royal Scots)	
	11th "		" (10 Officers 40 NCOs proceeded for 2 days instruction in trenches being attached to 11th Royal Scots)	
	12th "		" An enemy raid on the Trenches occupied by B Coy (11th Royal Scots) two heavy bombardments of a few mins each with ten minute interval of the whole Battalion line, then an attack on the Trenches occupied by B Coy (11th RS) by three parties of the enemy. Two were repulsed + a third gained access to the Trenches but withdrew after a short time, about 14 of the enemy not accounted for. Casualties in the Battalion were (2 Officers 5 NCOs +4 men) these Officers 2nd Capt G.P. Amery Stuart H.R. Pearse Stuart (I'm afraid) not recommended by C.C. 11th RS. for excellent work.	
	13th "		"	
	14th "		"	
	15th " 16th " 17th " 18th " 19th "		Gas alarm stood to 1-15 a.m. Stood from 1-50 a.m. (4 Officers 70 NCOs + men proceeded for 2 days instruction in trenches)	

WAR DIARY or INTELLIGENCE SUMMARY

Army Form C. 2118

Place	Date	Hour	Summary of Events and Information	Remarks and references to Appendices
PLOEGSTEERT WOOD	17th		Occupation of front line. Gas alarm 12.30 a.m. — No Gas over the Battn Area but the Tacquepot at PAPOT suffered slightly. During Enemy retaliation for our bombardment A + D Coys Clair suffered Casualties (3 killed 10 wounded).	
CRESLOW	18th		Billets at CRESLOW. Relieved at 5 a.m. by 21.K.R.R.C. Batta congratulated by C.O. for work in trenches.	
"	19th		" Rest day. At 11-45 p.m. Gas alarm given, no casualties. Patrol of 2 Lieut Higgins 1 N.C.O. & 4 men out from 7W.	
"	20th		" Gas over Battn Billets & no casualties. Patrol of 2 Lieut Higgins (1 N.C.O. 1 men) 2nd Patrol 1 N.C.O. 1 men out from 7W.	
"	21st		" Rest day. 1 Patrol out from T.112. 1 N.C.O. + 2 men from T.112.	
"	22nd		" Rest day. Patrol of 3 men out from T.112.	
"	23rd		" Rest day. Patrol of 1 Officer (2 Lieut Higgins) 2 men out from T.112. (1 casualty wounded)	
			Rest day. 11.30 p.m. Gas Alarm. No gas over Batt Billets. 2 Patrols out from "A" Coy T.111.	
			Rest Day. 2 Patrols out from "A" Coy T113 out of the line.	
CRESLOW	24th		Took over front line. Relieved 21.K.R.R.C. at 5 a.m. Patrols out as usual, one from front for photographs.	
PLOEGSTEERT WOOD	25th		Occupation of front line. Rest Day.	
"	26th		" D Coy Reed A boy in @ T. 113 - 115. Patrols out as usual, one of none (casualty arrested).	
"	"		" Patrols from T.112. Special Patrol returned.	
"	27th		" Rest day. Patrol of 3 men Sergt Leary out from T.113 met enemy patrol, bombs thrown. The of enemy seen to fall all over. Patrol wounded but got away. (Brownlie 1 killed 1 wounded)	
"	28th		" Rest day. Some Artillery fired on both sides. Patrol out from T.113 under Lieut Gates (Casualties 1 wounded).	
"	29th		" Rest day. Artillery fairly active (Officers 2/Lt PUGMORE, 2Lt KILMORE, & ...) preparation to front commenced.	
"	30th		" Artillery preparation to front commenced at 7-30 p.m. All arrangements completed for this. Fire successfully put in here & 6 lanes in enemy wire a 7113 drawing ...	

Army Form C. 2118

WAR DIARY
or
INTELLIGENCE SUMMARY
(Erase heading not required.)

Instructions regarding War Diaries and Intelligence Summaries are contained in F. S. Regs., Part II. and the Staff Manual respectively. Title Pages will be prepared in manuscript.

Place	Date 1916	Hour	Summary of Events and Information	Remarks and references to Appendices
LA CRECHE	20th May		In Billets at LA CRECHE.	
	21 "		" (4 Officers 50 N.C.Os men proceeded to 2 days instruction in trenches.)	
	22 "		" Committed suicide	
	23 "		" (1 Casualty No 19228 Pte H Evans self-inflicted about 2am) Court of Enquiry held Temporarily Insane)	
	24 "			
	25 "		"	
	26 "		"	
	27 "		"	
CRESLOW	28 "		Marched from LA CRECHE into Billets at CRESLOW	
	29 "		In Billets at CRESLOW	
	30 "		Moved up to Front Line. Took over trenches from 8th Black Watch (27 Brigade 9 Divn) Trenches 113-120, Right Batt⁰ Centre Sector. 11 Corps 11 Army. Left here to opposite "Birdcage" (1 casualty)	
PLOEGSTEERT WOOD	31 "		In occupation of Front Line A,B & C Coys in Firing Line & Supports. D Coy in Reserve (Bird Cage) Casualties NIL.	

_____
Lieut.-Colonel,
Commanding 15th (S) Battn. Hampshire Regt.

Army Form C. 2118

WAR DIARY or INTELLIGENCE SUMMARY

(Erase heading not required.)

Instructions regarding War Diaries and Intelligence Summaries are contained in F. S. Regs., Part II. and the Staff Manual respectively. Title Pages will be prepared in manuscript.

Secret XIX Vol 12

1/15 Bn. HANTS.

Place	Date 1916	Hour	Summary of Events and Information	Remarks and references to Appendices
PLOEGSTEERT WOOD	June 1st		Occupation of front line. About 10-20pm HQ at Rifle House shelled with 5.9 HE Grounds. Battery was demolished (F.F.) Casualties 1 killed 2 accidental	
	2nd		Returned to duty 3 wounded for the day	
	3rd		2 casualties (wounded) 1 casualty (wounded) Lieut Gates & Lt Patron on patrol, whilst inspecting enemy wire were observed and pursued by 6 of the enemy. They managed to evade them but were unable to return until 7.15am at which time a great risk they managed to get over parapet into our own lines at Rose House. 1 casualty (wounded)	
	4th			
	5th		Relieved from Trenches by 21st KRRC (124 Brigade) at 5 A.M.	
	6th		Quiet day	
	7th		"A" Coy shelled out of Billets in TOUQUET BERTHE, Barn that destroyed by fire & RE dump destroyed. (no casualties)	
CRESLOW	8th			
	9th		Quiet day	
	10th			
PLOEGSTEERT WOOD	11th		Relieved 21st KRRC at 5.8 P.M. Two patrols out from A & B Coys night 11/12	
	12th		Two patrols out from A + B Coys. night 11/12.	
	13th		Occupation of front line. Quiet. Patrols as usual at night	
	14th		Patrol of B Coy out for 24 hours 2 men (Pte Harris No 18479 & Cpl Hopkins No 9168) they brought in a bag of 3 enemy bombs, several cards of the enemy near HAMPSHIRE T. (Observing of enemy working?)	
	15th		Patrol of D Coy out for 24 hours near HAMPSHIRE T.	
	16th		Patrol of 2 men (Sergt Deary + A McCabe) went to BIRDCAGE when gas alarm started, they threw 10 bombs into enemy trenches. P in the dew.	

WAR DIARY or INTELLIGENCE SUMMARY

Army Form C. 2118

Place	Date	Hour	Summary of Events and Information	Remarks and references to Appendices
PLOEGSTEERT WOOD	Aug 30		Occupation of front line. Programme of Raid.	
		9.15pm	Artillery Bombardment commenced	
		9.45	" " ceased	
		10.0	Gas discharged	
		10.0½	Artillery Bombardment recommenced	
		10.2	Smoke discharged	
		10.15	Gas turned off	
		10.23	Raiding party started	
		10.25	Artillery lifts & raiding parties advanced	
		10.43	Raiding party reached enemy trench	
		10.53	Artillery ceased	
		1.25am	2nd gas discharge for 15 mts.	

Raiding party started in three groups M1 from the right under Lieut Green No 2 Bents under Lieut Jacob No 3 OP under Lieut Gale. No 1 reached the enemy trench & threw in bombs who owing to programme they had to return. No 2 lost its Lieut slightly wounded and 2nd bomb squad. No 3 worked along trench. Had some difficulty in getting through wire & returned. No party actually entered enemy trenches. The three of the relay in Lysloy [?] supply of bombs was much by no own gun. The had not stayed from the French Grenade on parapet & and caused delay to parties who had to put on gas helmets. Lieut Green killed. Lieut Knight died of wounds and Pte Penfold died of gas afterwards. 8 wounded & wounded.

Enemy retaliation on heavy. Lieut Gale got wounded. the Parry returned after the raiding parties had returned and brought in Lieut Greens body which was about 40 yds Jacobs.

Parties congratulated by G.O.C. 41 Division who said the object of the raid had been achieved viz to keep his enemies to his trenches & prevent him sending reinforcements elsewhere.

A number of recommendations was made for rewards for good work.
Casualties for whole day (9 killed. 28 wounded. 2 since died)

[Signed] Lieut. Colonel,
Commanding 15th (S.) Batin. Hampshire Regt.

41 Army Form C. 2118
15th Hants
July
12/41
Vol 3
345

WAR DIARY or INTELLIGENCE SUMMARY
(Erase heading not required.)

Army Form C. 2118

Instructions regarding War Diaries and Intelligence Summaries are contained in F.S. Regs., Part II. and the Staff Manual respectively. Title Pages will be prepared in manuscript.

Place	Date	Hour	Summary of Events and Information	Remarks and references to Appendices
PLOEGSTEERT WOOD & CRESLOW	July 1st	5 am	Relieved by 21/K.R.R.C. at 5 am. All day in Billets cleaning up and resting. Artillery on both sides active. Heavy Bombardment by us on Artillery at night in the Museum of ARMENTIERES	
	2nd		In Billets quiet day, routine + working parties	(1 casualty previously wounded DIED of wounds)
	3rd		" " " " " "	
	4th		" " " " " "	
CRESLOW & PIGGERIES	5th	10/30 pm	Batt'n moved to near our relieving 18 K.R.R.C. at PIGGERIES of one in support & 1 in reserve. Two Batts in lost and	
	6th		Quiet day in Billets. setting in working parties. Heavy Artillery bombardment at night by our guns attacked 250 (1st mile?) (Inft) RE	
	7th		" " " " " "	(1 killed 1 wounded attached 250 (Tunn?) Coy RE)
	8th		" " " " " "	
PIGGERIES & FRONT LINE	9th		Relieved 18 K.R.R.C. in Front Line Right "Battn" Left Sector Trenches (2 wounded (accidental) + 1 to duty) 125-129 inclusive. Raids by Batts. returning in night v 32nd R.F.	(1 casualty promoted)
	10th		Quiet day	
	11th		" "	
	12th		Artillery preparation all day for raid by 18 K.R.R.C. tonight. Some enemy retaliation. Raid of 18 K.R.R.C. unsuccessful. Rescue parties of this Batt'n went out to bring in wounded. Went forward while along the new killed (2nd Lieut Challis + Sgt Dunn specially mentioned for recommendation for the Military Cross for excellent work done on this occasion. (Casualties 1 killed 2 wounded Intelligence Summary)	(Casualties 1 killed 2 wounded Enemy Bomb work)
	13th		Artillery active all day. Gas attack from our lines during night. Rifle Grenade + Trench Mortars	
	14th		Enemy gas attack at 1 am. 2nd Lieut Challis killed + 3 men accidentally gassed (Hernalle 1st 2nd Grand)	
	15th		Quiet day except gas	
	16th		Quiet day. Some men of A Coy slightly gassed. This gas shivering in vomits + sniffing (7 gas casualties) back to trench.	
FRONT & PIGGERIES	17th		Quiet day. Battn relieved by 18 K.R.R.C. 7 moved into Billets at the PIGGERIES. Quiet day a few enemy shells near Billets.	

Army Form C. 2118

WAR DIARY
or
INTELLIGENCE SUMMARY
(Erase heading not required.)

Instructions regarding War Diaries and Intelligence Summaries are contained in F.S. Regs., Part II. and the Staff Manual respectively. Title Pages will be prepared in manuscript.

346
VB

Place	Date	Hour	Summary of Events and Information	Remarks and references to Appendices
PIGGERIES	18th		Quiet day a few shells over PIGGERIES	1 casualty
	19th		" " more shells closer to Billets.	3 casualties
PIGGERIES & ROMARIN	20th		G.O.C. 122 Brigade presented medal ribbons to Cpl. MURDEN & Pte PARRIS. (MILITARY MEDAL)	
	21st		out to G.H.Q. 2nd line fairly quiet a few shells over Billets. Batt. H.Q & B Coy removed to G.H.Q. 2nd line & Transport lines in evening C Coy removed at FOSSE LABARRE to	A&D Coys moved Billets shelled.
	22nd		Settling into new position in G.H.Q. 2nd Line. Transport lines & ROMARIN. Honours awarded. LIEUT GATES. MILITARY CROSS. Sgt DUGAN Pte BARTON Pte HEDGER Sgt PAGGETT & Cpl FISHER MILITARY MEDAL	
	23rd		Quiet day in Billets	
	24th		" " "	
	25th		" C Coy moved to G.H.Q line & "D" Coy went to FOSSE LABARRE	(2/Lt MARTIN died of wounds) 2nd T.M.B.
ROMARIN & CRESLOW	26th		Batt moved into Billets at CRESLOW	
	27th		Quiet day	
	28th		" "	
	29th		" "	
	30th		" "	
	31st		" "	

Ivan _____
Lieut. Colonel,
Commanding 15th (S.) Battn. Hampshire Regt

Army Form C. 2118

Vol 4

15 Hunts

WAR DIARY or INTELLIGENCE SUMMARY
(Erase heading not required.)

Place	Date	Hour	Summary of Events and Information	Remarks and references to Appendices
	AUGUST			
CRESLOW	1st		Quiet day	
	2nd		"	
CRESLOW & PLOEGSTEERT WOOD	3rd		Relieved 21st K.R.R.C. in trenches 113-120. A Coy went B night O centre B light continuing new H.R. Fairly quiet day. Enemy line treated with m.g. traverses + (Casualties. 2 killed 2 wounded) Patrols out as usual. 2/Lt MENZIES-CALDER + patrol after encountering many patrol scattered 2/Lt. N. CALDER who was out in the first line could only find two way back and ferreted out for 24 hours. It all probability he came in at T.135 at 11.30 p.m. on 4th stay in hiding. He came in at T.135 at 11.30 p.m. on 4th much valuable information obtained. He was slightly wounded.	
	4th			
	5th		Quite Quiet (an average of 100 Rifle Grenades put over into enemy line every day and caught largest (g towards) and enemy line every day and practically and offensive patrols out at night. Retribution from enemy (Casualties (2 wounded) Trench mortars, light + heavy co-operated in our general attacks.	
	6th			
	7th			
	8th			
PLOEGSTEERT WOOD & CRESLOW	9th		Relieved by 21. K.R.R.C. Went into Billets at CRESLOW. Proceeded to CRESLOW stood in afternoon. Boys moving to the subsidiary line	
	10th		Quiet day in Billets	
	11th		"	
	12th			
	13th			
	14th			
CRESLOW & LA CRECHE	15th		Batts. relieved by 8th York + Lancs Regt + marched to Billets at LA CRECHE.	
LA CRECHE & METEREN	16th		Batt. marched from Billets at LA CRECHE to Billets at METEREN.	
METEREN & FLETRE	17th		Batt. marched from Billets at METEREN to Billets at FLETRE.	

Army Form C. 2118

WAR DIARY
or
INTELLIGENCE SUMMARY
(Erase heading not required.)

Instructions regarding War Diaries and Intelligence Summaries are contained in F. S. Regs., Part II. and the Staff Manual respectively. Title Pages will be prepared in manuscript.

Place	Date	Hour	Summary of Events and Information	Remarks and references to Appendices
CRESLOW	AUGUST 1st		Quiet day	
	2nd			
CRESLOW & PLOEGSTEERT WOOD	3rd		Relieved 21st K.R.R.C. in trenches 113-120. A Coy reserve. B + C cents B Coy. Continuing new H.Q.	
			Fairly quiet day. Enemy fire normal. 2/Lt MENZIES-CHILDER + patrol out, with rifle grenades + (crowsfeet/trowelheads?)(Willies?) 2/wounded)	
			Patrols out as usual. 2/Lt MENZIES-CHILDER + patrol oft, encountered enemy patrol which did not fire, who was out in the front line until just before the daylight. He gained all his objectives but failed to reach well behind the enemy lines, saying that the whole area was at T.12.5 at 11.30 pm on bt. Much valuable information obtained. He was slightly wounded.	
	4			
	5			
	6			
	7		Quiet rough (very dry) average of 100 R/G Grenades put over into enemy line every day	
			Enemy fire (very dry) occurred + offensive patrols out at night. Retaliation from enemy practically nil. Trench mortars (light + heavy) co-operated in our French attacks.	
			Casualties (2 wounded)	
PLOEGSTEERT WOOD & CRESLOW	8		Relieved by 21 K.R.R. went into Billets at CRESLOW.	
	9		Rifled an afternoon. Boys moving to the subsidiary line.	
	10		Quiet day in Billets.	
	11			
	12			
	13			
	14			
CRESLOW & LA CRECHE	15		Battn relieved by 8th Yorks & Lancs Regt + marched to Billets at LA CRECHE.	
LA CRECHE & METEREN	16		Battn marched from Billets at LA CRECHE to Billets at METEREN.	
METEREN & FLETRE	17		Battn marched from Billets at METEREN to Billets at FLETRE.	

WAR DIARY or INTELLIGENCE SUMMARY

(Erase heading not required.)

Army Form C. 2118

Place	Date	Hour	Summary of Events and Information	Remarks and references to Appendices
FLETRE	18. 19/10 23		Training in Billets " " " " " "	
	24		Battn marched to BAILLEUL & entrained at 2-30 am 24th. Battn arrived at LONGPRE at 12-0 noon & detrained marched to Billets in VILLERS SOUS AILLY	
VILLERS SOUS AILLY	25 to 31		Training in Billets. " " "	

Harry Nannand Lieut.-Colonel,
Commanding 15th (S.) Hampshire Regt.

WAR DIARY
or
INTELLIGENCE SUMMARY
(Erase heading not required.)

Army Form C. 2118

Place	Date	Hour	Summary of Events and Information	Remarks and references to Appendices
FLETRE	18.		Training in Billets	
	19 to 23		" "	
	24		Battn marched to BAILLEUL & entrained at 2.30 am 24th Battn arrived at LONGPRE at 12.0 noon & detrained marched to Billets in	
VILLERS SOUS AILLY	25 to 31		VILLERS SOUS AILLY Training in Billets.	

[signature]
Lieut.-Colonel,
Commanding 15th (S.) Bn. the Hampshire Regt.

Army Form C. 2118

15th Hants.
122/4
Sep 1916.

WAR DIARY
or
INTELLIGENCE SUMMARY
(Erase heading not required.)

Instructions regarding War Diaries and Intelligence Summaries are contained in F.S. Regs., Part II. and the Staff Manual respectively. Title Pages will be prepared in manuscript.

Place	Date Sept	Hour	Summary of Events and Information	Remarks and references to Appendices
VILLERS-SOUS-AILLY	1. to 5		Training in Billets.	
DERNANCOURT	6	1.20 A.M.	Transport moved to DERNANCOURT, via LONGPRÉ (nr. AMIENS). Battalion marched to LONGPRÉ-LES-CORPS-SAINTS and entrained at 9.20 A.M. Battalion arrived at MERICOURT 9.15 P.M. detrained and marched to Camp at DERNANCOURT arriving at 1.45 P.M.	
	7 to 11.		Training in Camp.	
FRICOURT	11	3.15 P.M.	Battalion marched to FRICOURT via MEAULTE - BECORDEL. Arrived FRICOURT 5.50 A.M.	
	12	9 A.M.	Battalion moved to Trenches at MONTAUBAN, in reserve to 164th Bde. Coy. Officers & 4 Coy. Commanders visited front line between West of DELVILLE WOOD.	
		8 P.M.	Battalion returned to Camp near FRICOURT.	
TRENCHES W. of DELVILLE WOOD.	13.	6.15 P.M.	Batt. relieves 20th D.L.I. Relief complete by 8.15 A.M. 14th.	
	14.		Our Artillery very active all day. Shelling FLERS and BAPAUME.	
		11 A.M.	Moved 3/5 K. BADDELEY L. to Pt. Ass. Trenches two platoons Commence eccs of F.M. PARRY 10.20 P.M. 14/9/16. and.	
(ATTACK)	15.	6.20 A.M.	Action commenced with the Batt. moving down to an Advanced Pos. behind the barrage. The barrage in front of this Bn.T. was rather fast what the men had no chance to sufficiently so far satisfactorily in keeping the enemy quiet. Things were not so satisfactory on our left however for a few 10 mins. was later up before the Wiltshire came up there hitherto been allowed	

1875 Wt. W5393/826 1,000,000 4/15 J.B.C. & A. A.D.S.S./Forms/C. 2118.

WAR DIARY or INTELLIGENCE SUMMARY

Army Form C. 2118

(Erase heading not required.)

Three guns had heavy toll of the left platoon of Coy. Casualties to men - three being fatally hit before the first objective was won - Capt. H.E. CARRINGTON, Capt. E. THOMPSON and Capt. H. STAPLETON. One of these guns was put out by two men, who worked along the trench and shot the team.

The second objective was taken with our troops many of the enemy running towards FLERS without equipment or arms.

The enemy "barrage" was just up to their front, perhaps some along their forward troops rising to more or except where the BdR. with the 13th Bde. on the right and the 18th K.R.R.C. and the 12th except to THERS, which was entered and except in their elated and pursued faces.

Our new influence work behind our lines and our advance doubt unnerving in the enemy's front line and without doubt unnerving in the enemy, I also here the new great confidence has been fairly keen moving to the heavy barrage put up by the enemy through FLERS. By the time troops had engaged FLERS rigorously ahead had cleared pushing to formation having broken up and to heavy character amongst the officers. This appears to have resulted in men into shelving had broken through getting into dug outs, or digging in around and beyond the village. They were forced our and removed, and little or no information came back to BaR. H.Q.

WAR DIARY or INTELLIGENCE SUMMARY

Army Form C. 2118

Shrapnel barrage of Gas Barrage Shells was continued without sufficiency of HE shells and at first, when men were seen coming out of the trenches and taught to return, attack was in force, every man was ordered to lie down in some kind of cover, including shell holes. Two of the enemy's machine guns were masked and the Bn Bomber party with the RO left behind prepared to defend the trenches. The Bn HQ during the period moved by bounds from the Sunken Highway to the First Objective. After the Second Objective had been taken and again to the Second Objective after FLERS had been taken. It did not subsequently move here but its HQ was put forward to enter up the situation.

No message, however, began to come in after 11 AM, but it was not known how our Commanders were getting on, and no messages had reached us. Capt. Regt. Major wounded, his evening. This was followed by Capt. W. G. W. BAILEY. The Commander in front of the BCR was killed and the whole the Battn objective was taken, all survivors before this seems.

Meanwhile, the "MI" Brigade appeared to advance without sufficient artillery support. Their front line suffered on Lom Hell the Germany during the day. Rifle fire the Mr Rifle. The valley between the two was kept free for the fire, fired about every 20 minutes or so through the afternoon. The First indication of the winning of the particular operation of the escape was the withdrawal of the New Zealand Division on our left, who retired for a short distance and then started to dig in their boats. I saw aeroplanes went back into FLER and again offer, came out during the close of the firing, again when men were rushed forward but during the day the recessiny was in and of their bay barrage after the attempts had continued got into the village, and the Ocean. The matter of H. A. A.D.S.S./Forms/C.2118 Battn crept up to the Coventry,

WAR DIARY or INTELLIGENCE SUMMARY

Army Form C. 2118

The next morning 16th Corp (now Sergt) MURZEN reported that
Lt. Smith was with there with L. Coe. DRESSER (E Kerry?)
and Lt. Menzies Coe, took the latter being wounded
(once and the N.C.O. having been brought in the
balance of the party. The Officer was perfectly
with reference to the bullet wound, and nothing
done. The accuracy of the enemy barrage, however, that
nothing went to ground and the heavy barrage, however that
after we got to retire Turner Howie Smith
there the Regiment dropped. his to the enemy line Morris
Gunn. were captured were capturing two enemy Machine

The trench here was supplies with Mineral Water Cigars
and Bread. These were also a large number of Bombs
by Lt. 899 of Endicone ???. in the second fortnight that to any out.
It was noticed were half fuses of equipment & rifles,
20 feet deep.
Lt. SMITH, Lt. MENZIES. ORDER Lt. TOLLEMACHE & Lt. HALL all
advanced with guns parallel attention & bombarding to
heavy. He ??? out reports what had key been received with Lt. H.Q.
to furnish info ??? until last Lt TOLLEMACHE came wounded
had been unawares. his new ??? TOLLEMACHE accepted came wounded to
remained with village. and ??? ??? forwards to

CASUALTIES.   Officers   killed   8.
                        wounded 5.
              Other ranks
                        killed 31.
                        Missing 60.
                        Wounded 188.

S. Uncles. M.O.

Army Form C. 2118

WAR DIARY
or
INTELLIGENCE SUMMARY
(Erase heading not required.)

Place	Date	Hour	Summary of Events and Information	Remarks and references to Appendices
YORK TRENCH (RESERVE)	16.	7 p.m.	Battalion relieved from York and Reserve Trenches & placed in Reserve. York Trench. Enemy put five H.E. Shrapnel over on to Reserve trenches. – No casualties.	
TERNANCOURT	17.	6 a.m.	Battalion moved into Camp at TERNANCOURT arriving at 8.30 a.m.	
	18/		Training in camp. — Quiet in the area.	
	19/			
	30.		Training in Camp. — Quiet in the area.	

Hay Ramsal
Lieut.-Colonel,
Commanding 15th (S.) Battn, Hampshire Regt.
1st October 1918.

MARCH TABLE 122ND INFANTRY BRIGADE.

UNIT	DATE	TIME	STARTING POINT	ROUTE.
Brigade Headquarters Personnel	24-8-16	12.15 a.m.	Road Junction (W.6.t.3.7.)	FLETRE METEREN BAILLEUL (Rue de la Gare) MAIN STATION.
122nd Trench Mortar Battery.	24-8-16	12.17 a.m.	-do-	-do-
122nd Machine Gun Company.	24-8-16	12.20 a.m.	-do-	-do-
Horse Transport in order of March.	24-8-16	12.30 a.m.	-do-	-do-

Army Form C. 2118

WAR DIARY
or
INTELLIGENCE SUMMARY

(Erase heading not required.) HAMPSHIRE REG'T VOL 6

Page 1   15th

41st Div.

Remarks and references to Appendices

Place	Date	Hour	Summary of Events and Information
DERNANCOURT	Oct. 1st		Battalion in Camp at DERNANCOURT training and preparing to move up the line.
MAMETZ	Oct. 2		Battalion moved into bivouac at MAMETZ. Much rain. Roads in bad condition.
SOMME	Oct. 3		Battalion moved into the Line via THISTLE DUMP and TURK LANE. Disposition as follows A Coy on right, C Coy in centre, D Coy on left in GIRD LINE. B Coy in support in PIONEER LANE.
	Oct. 4		Soon after 5 A.M. the enemy delivered a bombing attack on the right of D Coy and left of C Coy., their objective was the high ground at the junction of the two companies. The attack was determined. and We defended ourselves with bombs and Machine Guns

WAR DIARY
or
INTELLIGENCE SUMMARY

(Erase heading not required.)

Army Form C. 2118

Place	Date	Hour	Summary of Events and Information	Remarks and references to Appendices
SOMME			July 2.	
	5.		Our aeroplanes had great opportunities. The attack appeared to be hung fire on the right however — left of the line towards the T.M. forward end. The attack was apparently not getting into touch with the Coldstream were ahead. 2 New recces were sent up to appearance. C. Party of one sign of the Battalion were hit. Party of 13 Bombers from the 16 K.R.R.C. Company at 2 Entrenching unit moved up on the left drawn up at 2.30 Consolidating and repairing the attack. The other of the Common & Trench. The left Common were moved the Common advance. They accordingly had Bombing countered & but in the case of the Common officers, and only occupied it, but out of the Bombing party 23 who had up the gap. The Bombing party of the same Regt. advanced up the line up to the Sap running between GR1 & GR2 SUPPORT that every time the self searching the trench around 60 yds. along to a point where the trench was blown in the party wanted two & water to his enemy to advance. Where their ompes threw them as they passed the opening. But keeping to enemy down he was able to study this trenches. Apparently two trenches was nearly full of Common & Snipers. The trenches around were full of Germans dead.	
	6.		At 3.15 a.m. an enemy bombing party who strong were in appearance in GR1 SUPPORT & attempted to bomb our towards they were easily driven back & pursued up the trench to where our 70 yards where he disappeared to advance for.	

Army Form C. 2118

WAR DIARY or INTELLIGENCE SUMMARY
(Erase heading not required.)

Page 3

Place	Date	Hour	Summary of Events and Information	Remarks and references to Appendices
SOMME	6		The enemy appeared to have no heart in this enterprise which ended up more like a foot race. An enemy working party was fired on by a Vickers Gun at a range of about 2300 yds and dispersed. An enemy party of about 4 men seen moving about in screen shapes like a landscape target and painted while one side was black the other, 300 yds from our front. A bombing party of this regiment the previous afternoon advanced from our front line up the sap running between GIRD trench and GIRD SUPPORT. What enemy there were occupying the trench retired before us to a point 60 yds along where the trench was blown in. We halted and as the enemy advanced again were able to snipe them as they crossed the blown in portion. We also shot down his flag – a black and red one. By keeping the enemy down for about an hour we were enabled to study his trenches. Apparently the trench is weakly held by bombers and snipers. The trenches around here are full of German dead.

General attack took place on the enemy.

Bombing took place on the 4th of October up to the GIRD and GIRD SUPPORT. At first we bombed up about 60 yds in the GIRD SUPPORT. Subsequently the enemy attacked and took back the whole of this advantage. A subsequent attack on our part left us in possession of about 20 to 30 yds of new ground. The Stokes Guns enfilading the GIRD trenches were most useful. They enfiladed the trenches and obviously contributed to the checking of the enemy. The enemy used the stick grenade and appeared to bring up a special party for the regaining of the trench when lost. The bombing attack was not so successful now the support partly due to a strong block with machine guns and the failure of the left of the line to take the trenches. Though of course the stick grenade is not such a good bomb as the Mills, it can be thrown further. | |
| | 7. | | On the afternoon of the 7th. when our attack in front of GIRD trench was held up by heavy Machine Gun fire, the enemy attempted a counter attack by bombing down that portion of GIRD trench which ran into our front line. During to the heavy casualties we had suffered the enemy above us step by step down GIRD trench towards our original front line and it looked almost as if [unclear] eventually penetrate into our trench. At this juncture Lieut. Pearsall 18th K.R.R.C. led a small party of– | |

Army Form C. 2118

WAR DIARY
or
INTELLIGENCE SUMMARY
(Erase heading not required.)

15th Hampshire Regt

347
/M/

Place	Date	Hour	Summary of Events and Information	Remarks and references to Appendices
SOMME	7.		Page 4 Hampshires and K.R.R. up the GIRD trench to meet the enemy and in spite of casualties drove them back and held them, blocking the trench when further progress was impossible. With his bombing party much reduced he held the barricade he had constructed against repeated attacks, and when he was finally wounded, the position had been firmly secured. Casualties in the Battalion this day: advanced to old trench ca. 290 to right 100 x on left. The day was spent consolidating the position gained on the 7th. The strong points were connected up and communication trenches dug to the old front line.	
	8			
	9		Battalion relieved by the 20th D.L.I. & 10th R.W.K. & proceeded to BROWN Trench. Day spent clearing up FISH ALLEY & BROWN trench.	
	10,11		Battalion proceeded to CASTLE YORK Trench, and cleaned up; and next day to EAST of MAMETZ WOOD on X 29 b central (approx) and proceeded to MEAULTE where it detrained	
DERNANCOURT	12		Battalion entrained at E.14.a via "fair weather" track and LEVEL CROSSING. and marched to the late Camp at E.14.a.	
	13-16		Battalion at rest in Camp. General reorganization; drafts from various regiments to the number of 388 had been received between 6th and the 12th.	
	17		Battalion entrained at MERICOURT for the ABBEVILLE AREA during the afternoon in two trains leaving about 3 PM and 5 PM respectively and 12.20 P.M. respectively, and proceeded to billets at Battalion detrained at OISEMONT at 11 AM and 12.20 P.M. respectively, and proceeded to billets at HUPPY.	
ABBEVILLE	18		HUPPY.	
	19		Training at HUPPY	
	20		Battalion entrained about 5.30 P.M. at PONT REMY for the SALIENT.	
YPRES SALIENT	21		Battalion detrained at CAESTRE and went into billets at EECKE.	
	22-23		Training at EECKE. A draft of 70 were received this day.	

1875 Wt. W593/826 1,000,000 4/15 J.B.C. & A. A.D.S.S./Forms/C.2118.

WAR DIARY or INTELLIGENCE SUMMARY

Army Form C. 2118

348

Place	Date	Hour	Summary of Events and Information	Remarks and references to Appendices
YPRES SALIENT	24		Battalion moved into billets in the MONT DES CATS area.	
	25		Battalion marched to ONTARIO CAMP, RENINGHELST.	
	26-28		Training in Camp. Special attention to new box respirators.	
	27		Battalion inspected by the 2nd Army Commander General Sir H. PLUMER G.C.M.G., K.C.B.	
	28		Camp inspected by Major General S. LAWFORD Commanding the 41st Division.	
	29		Battalion relieved the 23rd Middlesex Regt., 123rd Bde. in the ST ELOI Sector.	
	30		Line quiet.	
	31		Line quiet.	

Lieut.-Colonel,
Commanding 15th (S.) Battn. Hampshire Regt.

WAR DIARY
or
INTELLIGENCE SUMMARY

Army Form C. 2118

Vol 7

15th (Ser) Bn. Hants Regt.

November 1916.

WAR DIARY
INTELLIGENCE SUMMARY
(Erase heading not required.)

Army Form C. 2118

Instructions regarding War Diaries and Intelligence Summaries are contained in F.S. Regs., Part II. and the Staff Manual respectively. Title Pages will be prepared in manuscript.

Page 1

Place	Date	Hour	Summary of Events and Information	Remarks and references to Appendices
ST. ELOI	Nov. 1		Battalion in the line at ST. ELOI. Mining operation took place at 5.30 a.m. a Camouflet being exploded opposite No.3 Crater to interrupt enemy mining there. Operation successful, no crater was formed nor any damage done to our parapet. After the explosion the enemy sent up many Very lights and opened fire on our parapet with Machine Guns. The artillery were 'standing to' in case of development. Line otherwise quiet.	
	2		Enemy transport observed passing along MESSINES-YPRES ROAD about 2000 yds. from the right of our line (i.e. Trench O2.5). We opened fire with Lewis Gun and transport took cover in wood; information sent to our artillery and wood shelled. Line otherwise quiet.	
	3		Line quiet. Battalion relieved by 10th R.W.K. Regt., 123rd Inf. Bde. and moved to rest camp bivouac at QUEBEC CAMP, RENINGHELST.	
RENINGHELST	4		Battalion in camp. Cleaning up.	
	5		Battalion in camp. Church Parade 10.30 a.m.	
	6		Battalion on fatigues all day, camp deserted.	
	7 & 8		Battalion in camp. Very wet.	
DICKEBUSCH	9 & 10		Battalion in reserve: Half at VOORNEZEELE and remainder with H.Q. at DICKEBUSCH. Working parties have to be found daily chiefs for night work.	

WAR DIARY
or
INTELLIGENCE SUMMARY
(Erase heading not required.)

Army Form C. 2118

Page 2

Place	Date	Hour	Summary of Events and Information	Remarks and references to Appendices
DICKEBUSCH	Nov. 11, 12		Battalion in Reserve, A & C Coys at Voormezeele, H.Q. and B & D Coys at Dickebusch. Maximum number of men employed on night working parties for the R.E. and Pioneers. Small parties, totalling about 60 men, were also supplied for day work.	
	13	1 A.M. – 5 A.M.	The Half Battalion in VOORMEZEELE was relieved by that in DICKEBUSCH. Relief carried out by road via CAFÉ BELGE and completed before daybreak. Working parties chiefly for night work, were supplied.	
	14		Working parties were supplied, chiefly for night work.	
	15	11 A.M. – 11:30 A.M.	The enemy sent over about 15 shells of medium calibre, into DICKEBUSCH. A Coy of the 11th Queens, who were resting in DICKEBUSCH at the time, on their way to the trenches, suffered about 20 casualties, including 4 men killed and two officers wounded. The 15th Hauts' Stretcher Bearers and 2 officers' servants of "A" Coy were immediately on the spot and rendered every assistance. The morning was bright and clear, and it is supposed that the QUEENS' were seen by the enemy just before entering DICKEBUSCH. Working parties were supplied, chiefly for night work.	
CHIPPEWA CAMP – RENINGHELST	16		The Battalion was relieved by the 10th R.W.K., and moved into camp at CHIPPEWA CAMP, near RENINGHELST. Owing to the lack of accommodation H.Q. and most of the officers subsequently moved to QUEBEC CAMP, RENINGHELST.	
	17, 18		150 men employed on various working parties. Remainder of Battalion training in Camp.	

WAR DIARY
INTELLIGENCE SUMMARY
(Erase heading not required.)

Army Form C. 2118

Page 3.

Place	Date	Hour	Summary of Events and Information	Remarks and references to Appendices
CHIPPEWA CAMP — RENINGHELST	Nov. 19	10 a.m.	Church Parade in Y.M.C.A. Hut at RENINGHELST. Training in Camp during the afternoon.	
	20		Battalion in Camp. Presentation of medals, won on the Somme, by the Corps Commander during the morning. Remainder of day spent in training.	
	21		300 men on various working parties. Remainder training in camp.	
	22		300 men on various working parties. Remainder training in camp.	
ST. ELOI	23		The Battalion relieved the 23rd Middlesex Regt. 123 Inf. Bde., in the ST. ELOI sector. "B" Coy occupying the Right of the front line, with half "C" Coy in the "Mud Patch". "A" Coy occupied Old French Trench, "D" Coy VOORMEZEELE SWITCH, and the remainder of "C" Coy ECLUSE TRENCH. H.Q. remained at the dressing Station, VOORMEZEELE.	
	24	12 noon	The enemy shelled VOORMEZEELE with 12 ·77 shells and the front line with a few Trench Mortars. No damage was done. Otherwise the line was quiet.	
		2 PM	The enemy's heavy Trench Mortars and Rifle Grenades were active between our front and Support Lines in the vicinity of CONVENT LANE. No damage was done. Our medium Trench Mortars and 18 pounders shelled the enemy's lines, doing considerable damage to his trenches and wire.	
	25th	3 PM	The enemy retaliated with a few ·77 shells over our Reserve Trench. With the exception of a few Trench Mortars and small shells, fired on each side during the afternoon, the line was very quiet.	

WAR DIARY
INTELLIGENCE SUMMARY

(Erase heading not required.)

PAGE 4.

Place	Date	Hour	Summary of Events and Information	Remarks and references to Appendices
ST. ELOI	Nov. 25		The day was very wet and misty.	
	26	9.30 A.M.	Enemy bombarded our front and support lines. The parapet fell in in three places and four casualties were inflicted, including one man killed. The Artillery and Trench Mortars were fairly active on both sides throughout the day; especially at 3.30 P.M. when our Trench Mortars shelled No III Crater, blowing up a M.G. emplacement under construction.	
		3.30 P.M.		
		4.00 P.M.	"A" Coy; from OLD FRENCH TRENCH, relieved "B" Coy in the front line (Right sect$\frac{n}{r}$) and half "C" Coy; from ECLUSE TRENCH relieved the remainder of "C" Coy in the left sector of the front line. Various fatigue parties were supplied by "A" & "D" Coys in the course of the day, and "B" Coy continued to improve the drainage and revetment of the front line, until relieved by "A" Coy.	
	27		Listening and Reconnoitring patrols were sent out by "A" Coy during the night 26th/27th. Sounds of hammering were heard in the crater. Movement was found extremely difficult owing to the swampy nature of the ground. The enemy shelled our front and support lines at intervals throughout the day, causing no casualties and but slight damage to the front line parapet. Our Artillery retaliation on the craters was very effective.	
CHIPPEWA CAMP RENINGHELST.	28		The Battalion was relieved by the 10th R.W.K., and moved into CHIPPEWA CAMP near RENINGHELST.	
	29		Battalion in camp. Cleaning up.	

WAR DIARY or INTELLIGENCE SUMMARY

Page 5.

Place	Date	Hour	Summary of Events and Information	Remarks and references to Appendices
CHIPPEWA CAMP	30		Weather - Cold, turning to snow in the evening	
	31		Battalion in camp. Field Training (Scheme 3) carried out. Commanding Officers from 49th Inf. Bde. 16th Div. shown over 122nd Bde. Reserve Camps and B.H.Q. 2nd Line. Weather - Cold & fine. 3 Officers evacuated sick; 2/Lt Toogood (on course) 2/Lt Sergeant and 2/Lt Clarke. Names of 3 O.R. required for French Military Decorations. Pte Welch, Pte Merritt and Corp Stewart recommended, all for gallantry on the SOMME.	

Army Form C. 2118

WAR DIARY
~~INTELLIGENCE SUMMARY~~
(Erase heading not required.)

Page 5.

Instructions regarding War Diaries and Intelligence Summaries are contained in F. S. Regs., Part II. and the Staff Manual respectively. Title Pages will be prepared in manuscript.

Place	Date	Hour	Summary of Events and Information	Remarks and references to Appendices
CHIPPEWA CAMP RENINGHELST	Nov. 30		Battalion in Camp. 300 men were employed on various R.E. working parties. Remainder cleaning up the Camp.	

[signature]
Lieut. Colonel,
Commanding 15th (S) Battn. Hampshire Regt.

Army Form C. 2118

WAR DIARY
INTELLIGENCE SUMMARY
(Erase heading not required.)

Vol PAGE 1.

Place	Date 1916	Hour	Summary of Events and Information	Remarks and references to Appendices
CHIPPEWA CAMP RENINGHELST	Dec. 1	11.30 a.m.	Battalion in camp. Baths and training. At a representative parade the Commanding Officer distributed one Military Medal and several Divisional cards for gallantry on the SOMME, in SEPTEMBER. Three Officers and 300 O.R. on various working parties. Remainder of Battalion employed in cleaning up the Camp, and wiring in the parade ground.	SECOND ARMY No Q. 961 41st Dv. No Q 21/272
	2		The following message received from Second Army:— "Application has been received from 41st Division that the GERMAN HOTCHKISS MACHINE GUN No. 2327 captured by the 15th (Service) Battalion Hampshire Regiment on 7th October 1916 be allotted to this Battalion as a Trophy of War." This application is recommended. Instructions have been issued that the gun be properly labelled and despatched to the base.	
DICKEBUSCH AND VOORMEZEELE	3		The Battalion relieved the 23rd Middlesex Regt. in RESERVE. "A" & "C" Coys garrisoned VOORMEZEELE, under the Second in Command, and supplied garrison for SEPTEMBER POST (12 men and 2 Lewis Guns) and SPOIL BANK (Guard of 8 men). H.Q. and "B" & "D" Companies remained at DICKE BUSCH. The Battalion marched up by platoons at 100 yds interval, commencing at 7.30 a.m, and proceeding via OUDERDOM and MILLE-KAPPELEKEN FARM. The relief was effected without interference from the enemy. The Battalion supplied 4 Officers and 340 O.R. for various R.E. and Pioneer night working parties.	
	4	9 a.m	90 O.R. supplied for various R.E. working parties. Weather - Cold with a sharp frost. Day calm.	

WAR DIARY / INTELLIGENCE SUMMARY

Army Form C. 2118

PAGE 2.

Place	Date Dec.	Hour	Summary of Events and Information	Remarks and references to Appendices
VOORMEZEELE AND DICKEBUSCH.	4.		Four Officers and 347 O.R. supplied for various R.E and Pioneer night working parties.	
	5.	9 a.m.	50 O.R. on R.E. working parties.	
		2:30 p.m	The enemy sent over four shrapnell shells, one of which burst over the Y.M.C.A. No casualties were inflicted.	
			Four Officers and about 300 O.R. on various R.E. and Pioneer night working parties. Weather – Cold and dull with a few showers at intervals.	
	6.	9 a.m	50 OR on R.E. working parties.	
			The Battalion supplied 4 Officers and about 340 O.R. for various R.E., Pioneer and Tramway working parties (night). Weather - cold and dull; no rain.	
	7	9 a.m	59 OR on R.E. working parties.	
		10 a.m	A & C Coys in VOORMEZEELE were relieved by B & D from DICKEBUSCH. Four officers and about 300 OR on various R.E and Pioneer Night working parties.	
	8		The usual morning and night working parties supplied. Day Calm.	
	9		The Battalion was relieved by the 10th R.W.K., who commenced to arrive in DICKEBUSCH at 9:30 a.m. Companies moved out by platoons at 100 yds interval and marched to CHIPPEWA CAMP. Weather - wet.	
CHIPPEWA CAMP RENINGHELST.	10		Battalion in camp. Church parade 10:30 a.m. Route march during the afternoon.	
	11		80 men on various R.E. working parties. Remainder of Battalion training in camp, and baths.	
	12		The battalion, less the Specialists, on various working parties. Weather - cold, with some snow.	
	13		The battalion training in Camp. Weather Cold and fine.	
	14		The battalion supplied the usual working parties. Remainder training in camp.	

Army Form C. 2118

WAR DIARY
or
INTELLIGENCE SUMMARY
(Erase heading not required.)

Page 3.

Place	Date	Hour	Summary of Events and Information	Remarks and references to Appendices
ST. ELOI.	15		The Battalion relieved the 23rd MIDDLESEX, 123 BDE, in the line, the Companies being disposed as follows: ½ B in the MUD PATCH, ½ A and ½ D in the Right of the Sector, ½ B and ½ D in OLD FRENCH TRENCH, ½ A in ECLUSE TRENCH and "C" Coy in 'VOORMEZEELE SWITCH.' The day was comparatively calm in the line. Weather – Dull with occasional showers.	
	16.		The half Companies in the line were relieved by their opposites in Support. Day calm. Weather – fine and cold.	
	17.		Half Companies in the line relieved by their opposites in Support. Day calm. Weather – Very misty all day. No. 26901 Pte. Foster killed and 21740 Pte. Johnston wounded by Trench Mortar in MUDPATCH, the latter afterwards died of wounds on the 29th Dec. 1916.	
	18		Half Companies in the line relieved by their opposites in Support. Trench Mortars more active on both sides. Weather fine and cold. 2nd Lieut. A.E. Merritt was killed in the MUDPATCH. No. 26898 Pte. Swanton wounded, died later.	
	19		Half Company relief. Situation normal.	
	20		Half Company relief. Situation normal.	
	21		Half Company relief. Enemy's Artillery registered on all our trenches. Capt Mee was wounded in right wrist.	
CHIPPEWA CAMP RENINGHELST.	22		Battalion relieved by the 10th R.W.Ik, relief commencing at 1.30 p.m. Platoons marched out at 100 yds interval to CHIPPEWA CAMP, RENINGHELST. 4 Officers and about 300 O.R on various R.E. and Pioneer working parties. Remainder cleaning up.	
	23			
	24		Voluntary Church parade at 10.30 a.m. The Divisional Commander presented medals to NCOs and men for gallantry in the SOMME fighting during SEPTEMBER.	
	25		CHRISTMAS DAY. The Battalion paraded by Companies for baths. All Coys were provided with a Christmas dinner in the course of the day.	

WAR DIARY
INTELLIGENCE SUMMARY
(Erase heading not required.)

Army Form C. 2118

PAGE 4.

Place	Date DEC '16	Hour	Summary of Events and Information	Remarks and references to Appendices
CHIPPEWA CAMP.	26		A representative Coy. consisting of 65 O.R. from each Coy, and three officers, paraded for the Commanding Officers inspection and to practise Ceremonial drill for the Special parade on the 27th. Remainder training in Camp.	
	27		A representative Coy paraded for a Representative Corps Parade near BUSSEBOOM (R22 b) The Corps Commander distributed MONTENEGRIN honours to Brig. Gen. GORDON, 123 Inf Bde.; and other officers and W.O's	
	28		Training in Camp. Weather - Cold, with a sharp frost.	
DICKEBUSCH & VOORMEZEELE	29		The Battalion relieved the 23rd Middlesex Regt. in Reserve. A & C Coys. at VOORMEZEELE and B & D at DICKEBUSCH. Line quiet.	
	30		Artillery activity above normal on both sides. No. 10122 Pte. Gout wounded.	
	31		Further artillery activity. Number of officers on duty with Battalion now down to twelve. Nos. 25164 Pte. Wilkes, 20200 Pte. Spens, 27057 Pte. Totman, wounded at VOORMEZEELE in line. Total admitted to Hospital from sickness during the month, one hundred and sixteen.	

Hans Norman Lt Col
Comg 15th Hants M.R.

Army Form C. 2118

WAR DIARY
INTELLIGENCE SUMMARY
(Erase heading not required.)

Vol 9

15th (Serv.) Batt. Hampshire Regt.

War Diary for January 1919

WAR DIARY / INTELLIGENCE SUMMARY

Army Form C. 2118

Place	Date	Hour	Summary of Events and Information	Remarks and references to Appendices
DICKEBUSCH & VOORMEZEELE	Jan. 1		Battalion in Reserve, 'A' & 'C' Coys. at VOORMEZEELE, 'B' & 'D' at DICKEBUSCH. Day quiet. About 5.25 p.m. heavy bombardment broke out on both sides. It was apparently started by the enemy sending up red flares which were taken up by us as an S.O.S. signal. The shooting ceased about 6 p.m.	
	2		Inter-company relief. 'D' Coy. relieved 'C' and 'B' relieved 'A'.	
CHIPPEWA CAMP RENINGHELST	3		Battalion relieved by 10th R.W.K. and proceeded to Camp near RENINGHELST. Draft of 48 O.R. joined the Battn. Baths and training in camp.	
	4		Training in Camp.	
	5		Training in Camp, chiefly outpost scheme.	
	6		Battalion in training – field operations – Outposts. Eleven O.R. evacuated sick during the week. 3 Church Parade 11 a.m.	
	7		Battalion in training in afternoon.	
ST. ELOI.	8		Battalion relieved 23rd Middlesex Regt in the line. The enemy bombarded VOORMEZEELE SWITCH and neighbourhood of STRAGGLERS POST and the relief was delayed for 2 hours in consequence. Line quiet in evening. Weather – Overcast, brightening in afternoon. Observation very good.	
	9		Half-Company relief. Line quiet, with the exception of a few "minnies" over SHELLEY LANE and CONVENT LANE. 10 Officers and 87 O.R. on various R.E. working parties.	
	10		Half-Company relief. No flew a camaflet at 3.30 a.m. No action taken by enemy. L/Cpl Humphrey was killed in the front line. Situation – Normal. Reserve Coy on various R.E. working parties. Weather – Overcast.	
	11		Half Company relief. Line quiet. Weather – dull with occasional snow showers.	

WAR DIARY or INTELLIGENCE SUMMARY

Army Form C. 2118

Page 2

Place	Date Jan 15	Hour	Summary of Events and Information	Remarks and references to Appendices
St. Eloi.	12		Half-company reliefs. Enemy's T.M's and Artillery on both sides fairly active. Weather - wet and dull.	
	13		2nd Bttn Green H'ds killed by machine gun fire in "LOCALITY". Half-company reliefs. Day calm. Weather - wet and dull.	
	14		1/2 Coy evacuated dug-outs during night.	
	15		Half-company relief. Day calm. Weather - wet and dull; misty. Battalion was relieved by 10th R.W.K. "Blood". The relief was apparently discovered + the enemy shelled the front line communication trenches with trench mortars + minnie. A breech was made in the right half of the front line taken in CONVENT LANE. Two platoons of C Coy were cut off twice unable to relieve until dark. This was done without casualties the men arriving in camp at 9 p.m. that evening.	
CHIPPEWA CAMP RHENINGHELST	16		Battalion supplied 300 men for R.E. working parties. Remainder of battalion were trained in Camp. Snow fell during the night.	
	17		Baths at CHIPPEWA CAMP were allotted to the battalion. Remainder of the day was devoted to training +paying men. About four inches of snow fell during the day.	
	18		The Companies went for a route march in the morning +reconnoitred the ground they were to have a scheme on, on the following day. The weather was too bad for parades in the afternoon so the time was devoted to a general "clean up". It was inclined to snow all day but turned to rain.	

WAR DIARY or INTELLIGENCE SUMMARY

(Erase heading not required.)

Army Form C. 2118

Page 3

Place	Date	Hour	Summary of Events and Information	Remarks and references to Appendices
	19.		In the morning the battalion carried out a "Reconnaissance in force" scheme. The afternoon was devoted to the usual routine of training. The new bayonet Obstacle course was used for the first time. The weather was dull & very cold inclined to snow	
	20.		"A.C." & "D" Coy went for a route march in the morning accompanied by the band. "B" Coy devoted the morning to training in Camp. In the afternoon "B" Coy went for a six mile cross country run & the remaining Companies did their usual afternoon training. In the morning the Lewis Gunners were taken to the range. Weather: Dull very cold with occasional snow showers. 6 O.R. evacuated sick during week. "2 sent home to Cadet Schools.	
	21.		Church parade 10 a.m. Cross-country run by platoons in afternoon. Weather – Cold and fine.	
VOORMEZEELE & DICKEBUSCH.	22.		Battalion relieved the 23rd Middlesex in Reserve. Disposition. H.Q. and "A" & "C" Coys in DICKEBUSCH, "B" & "D" Coys in VOORMEZEELE. 3 Officers and 432 O.R. supplied for various working parties, chiefly night parties. Quiet in area. Weather – cold and fine.	
	23.		3 Officers and 432 O.R. supplied for working parties. A draft of 45 O.R. arrived and were distributed among the Companies. Weather – cold and fine.	
	24.		The usual working parties supplied (3 Officers and 432 O.R.) Area quiet. Weather – fine and cold.	

Army Form C. 2118

WAR DIARY
or
INTELLIGENCE SUMMARY
(Erase heading not required.)

Bge 4

Place	Date	Hour	Summary of Events and Information	Remarks and references to Appendices
VOORMEZEELE AND DICKEBUSCH	JAN 25		The usual working parties supplied. The enemy's Artillery shelled the Belgian Battery by DICKEBUSCH LAKE, firing about 200 shells. One gun was put out of action and 2 men wounded. Several Dug-outs were also damaged. The Commanding Officer took over the Command of the Brigade temporarily during the absence of the Brig.-Genl. at Divisional H.Q. Capt. Kendall assumed command of the Battalion, during the Colonel's absence. Weather – Cold & fine. Ice on small stretches of water now suitable for skating. Two new Officers from the 3rd (Special Reserve) Bn. joined the Battn. for duty.	
	26		The Half Battn. in VOORMEZEELE were relieved by that at DICKEBUSCH. Enemy's Artillery quite generally. Weather - Cold and fine.	
	27		The usual working parties supplied. Quiet in the Area. Officers and NCO's from the DICKEBUSCH Companies inspected G.H.Q. 2nd LINE and positions were allocated to Platoons. Weather – Cold & fine. The frost which has prevailed for over a week has rendered the ground hard enough to stand heavy transport. 3 OR. evacuated sick.	
CHIPPEWA CAMP	28		Battalion relieved by 10th R.W.K. Regt. and proceeded to CHIPPEWA CAMP. Weather - Cold + fine. 3 Officers and 202 OR on working parties. Remainder	
	29		Battalion in Camp.	
	30		Baths and training in Camp. Football match between officers and Sergeants at 2:30 p.m. 4 Battn. Sergeants 3. Officers 2 goals.	

WAR DIARY or INTELLIGENCE SUMMARY

Army Form C. 2118

15 Hamp Regt

PAGE 1. Vol 10

Place	Date 1917	Hour	Summary of Events and Information	Remarks and references to Appendices
CHIPPEWA CAMP.	FEBY 1		Battalion in Camp. 2 Officers and 150 OR on various working parties. Remainder training in Camp. Weather – Cold and fine. No signs of thaw.	
	2		Battalion training in Camp.	
ST. ELOI	3		Battalion relieved the 23rd Middlesex, 123 Bde, in the line. The relief was advanced by two hours and was completed without any casualties to the Hants. Disposition "B" & "C" Coys Right sector 015 – 029, half companies in the line and half in support. "D" Coy supply the "LOCALITY" Garrison, remainder in support. "A" Coy in Reserve in ECLUSE TRENCH. H.Q. at DRESSING STN, VOORMEZEELE. The Commanding officer returned to the Battn. Line quiet. Weather – no change.	
	4		Half company relief. Line quiet, with the exception of a few trench Mortars A Stray shell fell in vicinity of Coy HQ in Old French Trench, killing one man and wounding four. 104 OR on RE working parties. Half Company relief. Line quiet. Weather – no change.	
	5			
	6		Half Company relief. Reserved boy on R.E. working parties. Line quiet with the exception of a little trench mortar activity in the afternoon. Weather – Cold & fine	
	7		Half company relief. 104 OR – working parties for RE. Usual Trench Mortar activity during afternoon, otherwise line quiet. Weather, Cold & fine. Visibility very good during afternoon	

Army Form C. 2118

WAR DIARY or INTELLIGENCE SUMMARY

(Erase heading not required.)

Page 2.

Place	Date 1917	Hour	Summary of Events and Information	Remarks and references to Appendices
ST. ELOI.	FEBY. 8		Half-Company relief. 104 O.R. on R.E. parties. Line quiet. Weather - Cold and fine. 2/Lt LEYBOURNE rejoined the Bn. for duty.	
	9		Half Company relief. 104 O.R. on R.E. parties - Line quiet. Trench mortars (enemy) silent - for the first time during tour. Weather - Cold + fine. 2nd Lieut Williams slightly wounded. Evacuated to C.C.S. Battalion relieved by 10th R.W.K., and proceeded to camp near RENINGHELST.	
CHIPPEWA CAMP.	10.		Weather - Cold and fine. The Commanding Officer proceeded on leave, and was succeeded in the Command by Capt. H.P. KENDALL.	
	11		Church parade. Baths and Cleaning up. Weather - Cold and fine.	
	12.		About 140 O.R. on working parties. Remainder training in Camp. First signs of thaw, the weather breaking slightly.	
	13.		About 140 O.R. on working parties. Remainder training - Camp. The G.O.C. Brigade and Staff from XIth Corps inspected the camp and saw the men at work. Pte G.H. MERRITT awarded the CROIX DE GUERRE for gallantry on the SOMME. (At present in ENGLAND) 2/Lts H. PAGE, K. GRAHAM, and P.F. COLLIER reported for duty.	
	14		About 140 O.R. on working parties. Remainder training in camp. Slight thaw still continues.	

WAR DIARY

INTELLIGENCE SUMMARY

(Erase heading not required.)

Army Form C. 2118

PAGE 3.

Place	Date	Hour	Summary of Events and Information	Remarks and references to Appendices
CHIPPEWA CAMP.	15		2 Officers and 76 OR on working parties. Remainder training. Camp inspected by Gen. LAWFORD, accompanied by the Brigadier. General and Staff. Brig. Gen. LEGGE, from the X th Corps, also inspected the camp in the afternoon. Weather - Frosty night, followed by slight thaw.	
	16		2 Officers and 76 OR on working parties. Remainder Training - Outpost Scheme. Weather - slight thaw continues. Capt Wilkinson returned to duty - from hospital.	
	17		2/Lt Grant evacuated sick. The Battalion relieved the 10th R.W.K. in the line. Line quiet. Weather - dull.	
ST. ELOI.	18		Line quiet, with the exception of a little Artillery activity during the afternoon. The enemy's Artillery fired about 16 rounds in the neighbourhood of Bn H.Q. Weather - dull. Thaw continues.	
	19		Line quiet. No Trench Mortar activity. Weather dull and misty.	
	20		Trench Mortars on both sides very active during afternoon. Otherwise line quiet. Weather - dull and misty. Capt. Wilkinson assumed command of the Battn., vice Capt Kendall evacuated sick.	
	21		During the afternoon our Artillery and Trench Mortars cut the enemy's wire in front of the Craters. Retaliation poor. Weather - very misty. 2/Lts GORMAN, COOPE and KEEPE and 8 OR joined for duty.	
	22		Battalion relieved by 10th R.W.K. in the line. Relief delayed on account of proposed Bombardment of the enemy's trenches in rear of the Craters. The Bombardment was postponed owing to the fog.	

WAR DIARY

INTELLIGENCE SUMMARY

Page 4.

Place	Date	Hour	Summary of Events and Information	Remarks and references to Appendices
CHIPPEWA CAMP.	22.		The Battalion left the line without having suffered a single casualty.	
	23.		"A" + "B" Coys - Baths and Rest. "C" + "D" Coys - supplied working parties - Total. 1 Officer and 107 O.R. Weather - foggy.	
	24.		"C" + "D" Coys - Baths. Remainder training in Camp, + working parties.	
	25.		99 O.R. on various working parties; remainder training in camp. Weather - dull. The Commanding Officer returned from leave.	
	26.		1 Officer and 137 O.R. on various working parties. Remainder training in camp. Weather - fine.	
S'ELOI	27.		The battalion relieved the 10th R.W.K. in the line. Disposition. A and D Coys in Right Sector (0.25 to 0.28). Half Coys in line and half in support. B Coy supplying garrison of LOCALITY with remainder in support in OLD FRENCH TRENCH. C Coy in reserve in ECLUSE TRENCH.	
	28		Enemy artillery active. During the morning he shelled our supports and in the afternoon Voormezeele. For two hours after daylight a considerable amount of sniping was done on both sides, in the afternoon his trench mortars commenced shelling our front line but caused when retaliation was given by our Stokes. 2/Lt L.J. Johnson joined for duty, and was posted to "C" Coy. No 2 9215 Pte Downing R. who about 10 to...	

WAR DIARY or INTELLIGENCE SUMMARY

Army Form C. 2118

1/5 Manch. Regt. 22/4/

Place	Date	Hour	Summary of Events and Information	Remarks and references to Appendices
ST ELOI	1/3/17		Enemy artillery active. Our front, supports and reserves being shelled during the morning but we suffered no casualties from this shelling. During the afternoon the weather became very clean and consequently our aeroplanes were very active. At about midnight Pt. 27501 J.W. Shade of B Coy was wounded in the head while on sentry in Lekenring Post in the LOCALITY.	
	2/3/17		At intervals during the whole day enemy shelled our front line, supports and reserves but inflicted no loss to us. Our trench mortars shelled the enemy during the morning, but their retaliation was small. Weather fairly clean.	
	3/3/17		Kept up the shelling of SHELLY FARM. Enemy artillery were very quiet. Our men working under R.E's and wiring party in ECLUSE TRENCH was shelled to DICKEBUSCH to make room for a company of 1st K.R.R. Weather, moderate during first part of morning, fine clearer afterwards.	
			Enemy active but not heavy. Our front line, supports and Batt. H.Q. only received a few casualties during our counter battery work. P.E. 2750, Shade B. 24612 Slaunch the day. They were hit. 40/6 number 8/96, 1695 Green H. and P.E. 2750, Shade B. 24612 Slaunch and 69/shend. P. They all had bullet wounds. Our men were active on both sides all day. Weather was very clean all day.	
	5/3/17		Very little... Middlesex Regt. "D.O.W" shelled our trenches and...	

WAR DIARY or INTELLIGENCE SUMMARY

Army Form C. 2118

Place	Date	Hour	Summary of Events and Information	Remarks and references to Appendices
YPRES RAMPARTS CAMP	7.3.17		Battalion supplied 120 for R.E. Working Parties — Coms. B Coy carried out a scheme demonstrating the new form of attack. Not much doing in K.R.R. lines.	
	8/3/17		Battalion supplied 50 for R.E. Working Party. Coms. of Bn. attacked A and B Coy carried out the scheme. At 6.30 p.m we were ordered to "Stand by" as the enemy had shelled our trenches on the 16 Division front but at 7.30 pm the orders were cancelled.	
CHIPPEWA CAMP	9.3.17		Battalion supplied 164 for R.E. Working Party — Companies doing General training — Weather — Snow at intervals during day	
CHIPPEWA CAMP	10.3.17		Battalion supplied 20 for R.E. Working Party. Weather — Milder.	
VOORMEZEELE & DICKEBUSCH	11.3.17		Battalion relieved the 10th R.W.K. Regt 123 Inf Bd. Disposition. H.Q and 'B' & 'D' Companies in Dickebusch. 'A' Company in Ecluse + 'C' Company in Voormezeele. The weather was — very mild, sunny + clear and an engagement between several of our and the enemy's aeroplanes was visible, in which two of our machines were brought down, the third one escaping. The fight taking place in the Ypres direction. 4 officers + 215 o.R. supplied for various Working Parties. A Cpl had two casualties on the working party. They were 19581 L/Cpl Norman A + Drummer Shepherd G.	

1875 Wt. W593/826 1,000,000 4/15 J.B.C. & A.   A.D.S.S./Forms/C. 2118.

WAR DIARY
or
INTELLIGENCE SUMMARY
(Erase heading not required.)

Army Form C. 2118

Place	Date	Hour	Summary of Events and Information	Remarks and references to Appendices
VOORMEZEELE & DICKEBUSCH	12.3.17		3 Officers and 265 O.R. were supplied for working parties. Area - Quiet. Weather - Showery - Mild Temp.	
D°	13.3.17		4 Officers and 275 O.R. were supplied for Working Parties. Area Quiet. Weather - Showery - Mild. C.Coy were engaged all day in building Dug Outs in McGee Trench — Middlesex Lane.	
D°	14.3.17		3 Officers + 255 O.R. C. Coy supplying 2 Officers + 156 O.R. for work in McGee Trench, carrying for D.O. and retaining portion of Com H.Q. on Convent Road. A Patrol consisting of 2nd Lieut Fowler, Cpl Stuart + Ptes Dicks, Lunchene, Rappie, Naylor, Kelly, Rolland, Harris, Cross + L/Cpl Copping left our trenches at 8.P.M. for the purpose of placing two Bangalore torpedoes in the enemy's wire; was successfully carried out. Owing to one of the fuses breaking only one torpedo was fired, which was done at 10.30. The whole party returned safely. The object of this work being to detract the attention of the enemy, during a raid being made by the East Surreys of the same Bde, in which the artillery Rere cooperated. B Coy relieving C Coy and D Coy Relieving A Coy. Weather slight showers in morning afternoon Sunny Clear	

Army Form C. 2118

WAR DIARY
or
INTELLIGENCE SUMMARY

(Erase heading not required.)

Instructions regarding War Diaries and Intelligence Summaries are contained in F. S. Regs., Part II. and the Staff Manual respectively. Title Pages will be prepared in manuscript.

Place	Date	Hour	Summary of Events and Information	Remarks and references to Appendices
VOORMEZEELE & DICKEBUSCH	15.3.17		3 Officers + 255 o.R. were supplied for various working parties from A.C.&D Coys. B. Coy supplying 30 N.C.Os + Men for Carrying Parties - Trench floors, Tramways + Wiring. Middlesex Lane. Weather. Rain in morning. Fine with crusher later. Area Quiet	
Do	16.3.17		A patrol under the command of 2nd Lieut Bird went out from our trenches at 8.15 p.m. to try and find the fuse of the Bangalore Torpedo, which had been placed under the German wire on the night of the 14th + did not explode (being faulty), but after a thorough search not the slightest trace of it could be found. The patrol returned safely at 9.30 p.m. The men of the patrol were Ptes Harris and Rowland. 3 Officers + 261 o.R. were supplied for various working parties from A.C.&D Companies. B. Coy supplying 3 Off + 98 o.R. for various works in Voormezeele Switch McGee French Middlesex Lane for Carrying + Wiring &c. Area Quiet	
Do	17.3.17		The Battalion were relieved by the 23 Middlesex. Weather Fine Sunny + Mild Temp. Area Quiet	20 o.R. supplied for Working Party at YPRES GAS WORKS.

WAR DIARY or INTELLIGENCE SUMMARY

Army Form C. 2118

(Erase heading not required.)

Instructions regarding War Diaries and Intelligence Summaries are contained in F.S. Regs., Part II. and the Staff Manual respectively. Title Pages will be prepared in manuscript.

Place	Date	Hour	Summary of Events and Information	Remarks and references to Appendices
CHIPPEWA CAMP	18.3.17		Church Parade at 10.30 a.m. And cleaning up Camp. The Battalion was inspected by the Divisional Commander who commented on the smart & clean appearance of the men after being only one day out of the line. Weather Showery	
Do	19.3.17		Battalion training in Camp. Weather fine. 5 Officers and 60 men of the Battalion attended on the Parade Ground when the Divisional Commander presented Military Honours.	
Do	20.3.17		20 O.R. were supplied for R.E. Working Party. Weather fine morning, wet afternoon. A.C. Companies were occupied during the morning practicing the new scheme for open warfare and in the afternoon went through a special Course of GAS at the Divisional Gas School at Reninghelst.	
Do	21.3.17		B. & D. Companies also did the same Course of GAS in the morning and practiced the Scheme during the afternoon. The Batt'n Transport was inspected by the O.C. 4th Div'n from at 3 o'clock p.m. A draft consisting of 1 Officer (Lieut W.G. Wright) and 31 o.R. joined the Batt'n this afternoon & were distributed amongst Companies. Weather Moderately fine. Col'd winds	

Army Form C. 2118

WAR DIARY
or
INTELLIGENCE SUMMARY
(Erase heading not required.)

Instructions regarding War Diaries and Intelligence Summaries are contained in F. S. Regs., Part II. and the Staff Manual respectively. Title Pages will be prepared in manuscript.

Place	Date	Hour	Summary of Events and Information	Remarks and references to Appendices
CHIPPEWA CAMP.	22.3.17		The Battn was engaged in General Training during the morning and at 2 o'clock paraded with drums & marched to new Y.M.C.A. Hut at Reninghelst to attend performance of Pantomime (Aladdin) given by the Dicky Birds, which was much appreciated. Weather - Cold Wind & snow	
St Eloi	23.3.17		The Battn relieved the 10th Battn. R. W. Kent Regt in the line. Various working parties were employed and Reconnaissance Patrols went out at night. Weather fine. Disposition of Companies. A Coy Locality. B. Coy Reserve. Eclose Trench C. Coy Old French Trench & Right Sector. D Coy Voormezeele Switch & Right Sector.	
"	24.3.17		During the day the line was fairly quiet but towards evening there was more activity when French Mortars of both sides were engaged and at about 7.30 pm the Battn on our left were raided by the enemy. The Battn suffered one casualty in Pte Eldridge 10942 who was killed. The Clock was advanced one hour at 11 P.M. Weather fine. Various Working Parties supplied.	
"	25.3.17		The enemy Artillery was more active today & dropped about 8 Field Howitzer Shells in Voormezeele but did no damage, with the exception of very slightly wounding 19202 Pte Burton who remained with his unit. Otherwise the line was quiet. 27502 Pte Russell was also wounded. A draft of 40 O.R. joined the Battn which were distributed amongst the Companies. Weather fine. Working Parties supplied.	

WAR DIARY

INTELLIGENCE SUMMARY

(Erase heading not required.)

Army Form C. 2118

Place	Date	Hour	Summary of Events and Information	Remarks and references to Appendices
St. Eloi.	26.3.17		Line quiet, with exception of little Trench Mortar work were duly supplied. Reconnaissance Patrols went out at dusk. The usual Working Parties Weather was raining with cold wind. We suffered 3 Casualties in 27305 Pte Gosnell 25854 Pte Gates 27014 Pte Woodstock and Pte Slater 20973 all wounded.	
"	27.3.17		Line Quiet. At night one of Patrols went out & discharged a Sniping Post in NO MAN'S LAND. 24052 Pte Fleming and 19058 Pte Rook were wounded. Weather cold with slight snow. Working Parties supplied.	
"	28.3.17		There was Trench Mortar Activity in the morning & afternoon. We suffered casualties 18209 Pte White 22478 Pte Whitfield 27793 Pte Vine and 26199 Pte Hickman wounded and 18018 Pte Stoneham killed, three of which were caused by one of our shells falling short. Weather fine. The usual Working Parties were supplied.	
"	29.3.17		Line quiet. Capt. Barber reported for duty. Working Parties supplied.	Casualty 26991, Pte Collis, killed. Weather - rainy.

Army Form C. 2118

WAR DIARY or INTELLIGENCE SUMMARY

(Erase heading not required.)

Instructions regarding War Diaries and Intelligence Summaries are contained in F. S. Regs., Part II. and the Staff Manual respectively. Title Pages will be prepared in manuscript.

Place	Date	Hour	Summary of Events and Information	Remarks and references to Appendices
ST ELOI	30.3.17		The Battn. were relieved by the 23rd Batt. MIDDLESEX which was carried out without any casualty, and marched back to Chippewa Camp. 8.O.R. for R.E. Working Party were supplied. Weather fine. During the tour we had 3 men killed & 11 wounded.	
CHIPPEWA CAMP	31.3.17		Training of Companies and cleaning up Camp. 20. O.R. were supplied for R.E. Working Party. Weather Showery.	

C.L.531

From:-
   Officer Commanding,
     15th Hampshire Regt.

To:-
   Headquarters,
     122nd Infantry Brigade.

Please find enclosed War Diary for the month of April.

_____ Lieut.-Colonel,
Commanding 15th (S.) Battn. Hampshire Regt.

1/5/17.

Army Form C. 2118

15 Hampshire

5/12

WAR DIARY

~~INTELLIGENCE SUMMARY~~

(Erase heading not required.)

Place	Date	Hour	Summary of Events and Information	Remarks and references to Appendices
CHIPPEWA CAMP	1.4.17		Various R.E. Working Parties were supplied, the remainder of the Battⁿ undergoing training and also working in Camp. Weather fine	
Dº	2.4.17.		The Battⁿ were allotted the Baths for which Companies paraded accordingly and doing training in Camp the remainder of day. Weather. Snow in afternoon	
Dº	3.4.17.		During the night and until 10.30 a.m today there was a blizzard, but no damage was done in Camp, during the rest of the day weather finer, when training in Camp and work was carried on.	
Dº	4.4.17.		The Battⁿ supplied various R.E. Working Parties the remainder being engaged in training & work in Camp. Weather fine	

WAR DIARY
INTELLIGENCE SUMMARY

Army Form C. 2118

Place	Date	Hour	Summary of Events and Information	Remarks and references to Appendices
DICKEBUSCH	5.4.17		The Battⁿ relieved the 10th R.W. Kent Reg^t in Reserve. Disposition of Companies – H.Q, A & C Companies in Dickebusch. D. Co^y Voormezeele & B. Co^y September Post. Area quiet. Weather Fine – sunny & warmer.	
"	6.4.17		Various R.E. Working Parties were supplied. The Battⁿ supplied various R.E. working parties. Major Anceny M.C. returned to the battalion from England. Weather Fine. Area was shelled during most of the day.	
"	7.4.17		R.E. working parties were supplied. The Adjutant Capt Argimore returned after reporting his illness. Weather Showery. 41912 L/Cpl Davison raided the enemy lines on our left, 2/Lieutenant being taken and 27199 Pte Hobbs M^d to 27089 Pte Millingan and 253.41 Pte Baker. Twp attached to "D" Co. in Tunnelling Co was buried by mine explosion, the bodies have not yet been recovered. 122 T.M.B. killed	
"	8.4.17		The usual working parties supplied. Sgt 27498 Brooker W.E. also wounded by a shell at ??. Weather fine.	
"	9.4.17		Artillery activity again today. 27034 Pte Wiseman was wounded and 26879 Sergt Richardson gassed. 26958 Pte Annis The usual Working Parties were supplied. Weather Cold wind & snow	
"	10.4.17		Area quieter today the artillery activity being less than past few days. 26958 Pte Annis wounded Usual R.E. Working Parties were supplied. Weather cold & showery	
"	11.4.17		The Battⁿ supplied the various R.E. Working Parties required. Area fairly quiet again today 26651 Pte Hall was gassed. Weather cold & showery	

WAR DIARY
INTELLIGENCE SUMMARY
(Erase heading not required.)

Army Form C. 2118

Instructions regarding War Diaries and Intelligence Summaries are contained in F. S. Regs., Part II. and the Staff Manual respectively. Title Pages will be prepared in manuscript.

Place	Date	Hour	Summary of Events and Information	Remarks and references to Appendices
DICKEBUSCH	12.4.17		The Battⁿ supplied various R.E. Working Parties. 27060. Pte Windebank was wounded. Area fairly quiet. Weather Showery. 27060. Pte Windebank was wounded.	
" & CHIPPEWA CAMP	13.4.17		The Battⁿ was relieved by the 10ᵗʰ QUEENS and marched to Chippewa Camp where the remainder of the day was spent in cleaning up. Weather Fine and warmer. 2ⁿᵈ LIEUT. E.M.TREVETT evacuated sick. Met with accident in while he hurt his foot.	
CHIPPEWA CAMP	14.4.17		26972. Pte Lee slightly wounded at duty. Various Working parties were supplied. Companies being engaged in General training during the morning, the afternoon being granted as a holiday. Weather fine.	
"	15.4.17		The Battⁿ were allotted the baths for which Companies paraded accordingly. Various Working parties were supplied. Weather Raining all day.	
"	16.4.17		Various Working Parties supplied. Companies doing General training during day. Weather fine during day. Raining in evening.	
"	17.4.17		Various Working Parties were supplied. General training being carried out by Companies. A draft of men joined the Battⁿ & were distributed amongst Companies. Captⁿ Carr accompanied this draft & duly reported for duty. Weather fine.	

Army Form C. 2118

WAR DIARY
or
INTELLIGENCE SUMMARY
(Erase heading not required.)

Place	Date	Hour	Summary of Events and Information	Remarks and references to Appendices
ST ELOI.	18.4.17		The Battalion relieved the 26th R.F. (DEV) in the line. The dispositions of Companies being :- B Coy Right sector to OLD FRENCH TRENCH, C Coy. Right sector to O.F.T., D Coy locality to A Coy in Reserve. A general reconnaissance patrol went out from our trenches. Area quiet. Weather :- Rain & sleet.	
"	19.4.17		The enemy T.M.s were active during the day to which our Artillery & Stokes guns replied with much effect. A great deal of material from the craters being hurled into the air. Damage to our trenches Nil. We blew a camouflet at 6.50 A.M. with success to which there was no retaliation. Weather :- Showery.	
"	20.4.17		A quiet day in the line until 7.30 p.m when the enemy started shelling the right sector of our front line the front line of the 11th R.M.K who were on our immediate right. The shelling eventually developed into a heavy bombardment of our front & support lines during which the enemy twice attempted to raid our trenches but on each occasion	

Place	Date	Hour	Summary of Events and Information	Remarks and references to Appendices
ST ELOI	20(4)		never got further than his own wire being driven back by our L.G. fire & artillery barrage which on both occasions caught him just as he was leaving his trenches. This was entirely due to the fact that Capt. C.A. Barker, then in command of the right sector of our front line, sent up the S.O.S. light signal, (all telephones wire were dis.), at precisely the right moment when the enemy were leaving their trench. The garrison of our trench put up a vigorous defence and in spite of the heavy bombardment on our trenches the casualties were slight. Considerable comparatively damage was done to our trenches and a breach of about 100 yards was made in our front line. This however was speedily repaired. By the 23rd the sector of trench on either side of the breach were connected up again. The communication trenches were blocked in several places the support line, OLD FRENCH TRENCH, had also been blown in. This damage however was repaired within 24 hours. The enemy's objective was undoubtedly the mine shaft at the back of O.2.7.	

WAR DIARY or INTELLIGENCE SUMMARY

Army Form C. 2118

Place	Date	Hour	Summary of Events and Information	Remarks and references to Appendices
ST ELOI.	20/4/15		The enemy succeeded in penetrating the front line of the 11th R.Y.K. on our right. A few of their men were missing. About 25 O.R. were wounded. The following NCO's & men killed :- 27662 Pte Davis. 27782 Pte Viney. 27024 L/Cpl Rutler. 18463 Pte Williams 17597 Cpl Rogers. Weather :- Fine.	
do.	21/4/15		A quiet day in the line. Work of repairing our damaged trenches was speedily got on with. Weather :- Fine.	
do.	22/4/15		Our artillery bombarded the enemy's front lines on our right from 3 p.m. to 3.20 p.m. Considerable damage was done to his works. Otherwise area was quiet.	

Place	Date	Hour	Summary of Events and Information	Remarks and references to Appendices
ST ELOI	22/4/		Two patrols went out from our trenches in the early morning of the 22nd. One of the patrols went out with the object of inspecting the old cap, opposite O.29, in the enemy's line. The other patrol consisting of 2Lt D. Gorman, Cpl Anagon & Pte Harris went out with the object of bringing in an enemy casualty for purpose of reidentification. The patrol left our trenches from O.2.8 at 1.35 A.M. worked towards O.2.6 where they eventually entered our trenches again at 4.5 AM. During the patrol they encountered an enemy patrol in the middle of No Man's Land opposite O.2.7 working towards O.2.6. Our patrol got within 30 yards of enemy & threw bombs the enemy retaliated with rifle fire. The enemy patrol consisted of from 6 to 8 men. Our patrol returned safely.	

WAR DIARY or INTELLIGENCE SUMMARY

Army Form C. 2118

Place	Date	Hour	Summary of Events and Information	Remarks and references to Appendices
ST ELOI	23.4.17		The Battalion were relieved by the 26th Battn. R.F. and marched back to Chippewa Camp. During the relief, the enemy were the remainder of the day was spent in cleaning up. During the relief, the enemy dropped shells at Shrapnel Post Convent Wall, Victoria Street, Voorwezeele - no damage was done. (parts of) Weather fine.	
CHIPPEWA CAMP	24.4.17		The Battalion were allotted the baths for which the Companies duly paraded. The Battn. were paraded at 3.p.m. when the O.C. addressed the men and more especially to the men in the front line their good work in the line during the last tour and more especially to the men in the front line (C.Coy) who so gallantly held their position when the enemy attempted a raid on a two Battn. front (The R.W. Kent & ourselves) on the night of the 20th & when after three attempts did not gain any footing in those trenches held by this Battalion. A letter was sent to the Battn. by the Divisional Commander thanking them for their good work & sending them an invitation to an entertainment by the Div. Troops & also to the men in C. Coy who held the line. Weather fine.	

Army Form C. 2118

WAR DIARY
or
INTELLIGENCE SUMMARY
(Erase heading not required.)

Instructions regarding War Diaries and Intelligence Summaries are contained in F. S. Regs., Part II. and the Staff Manual respectively. Title Pages will be prepared in manuscript.

Place	Date	Hour	Summary of Events and Information	Remarks and references to Appendices
CHIPPEWA CAMP & BEAUVOORDE	25.4.17		The Battalion with its transport, forming part of the 122ND BRIGADE commenced the march back to Rest billets, moving off from Reninghelst at 9.30 a.m. marching through Boeschepe to Abele to Beauvoorde (on the Poperinghe Cassel road) which completed the first days march. Distance about 7 English miles from Chippewa Camp. Through the goodness of the P.R.I. Footballs were distributed amongst H.Qs and Companies respectively + matches were played in the afternoon which was given for recreation. Weather. Fine.	
BEAUVOORDE	26.4.17.		H.Qs & Companies went for a 5 mile route march in the morning. The afternoon was granted a holiday + football matches were played between H.Qs. Married v. Single + also between the Companies. Weather Fine.	
"	27.4.17		Battalion moved off again this morning at 9.30 a.m. the route being through Steenvoorde + Cassel to Ledringzele where billets were allotted for the night. Distance about 14 English Miles. Weather Fine.	
LEDERZEELE				

Army Form C. 2118

WAR DIARY
or
INTELLIGENCE SUMMARY
(Erase heading not required.)

Instructions regarding War Diaries and Intelligence Summaries are contained in F. S. Regs., Part II. and the Staff Manual respectively. Title Pages will be prepared in manuscript.

Place	Date	Hour	Summary of Events and Information	Remarks and references to Appendices
LEDERZEELE To TOURNEHEM	28.4.17		The Battalion moved off at 9.30 a.m. Passing through Watten & Nordausques to Tournehem which completed the march through duly billeted. Distance about 13 English miles. Weather fine.	
TOURNEHEM	29.4.17		Companies paraded for General Training and also Church Parade during the day. Weather fine.	
do	30.4.17		A & B Companies marched to Rifle Range in Training Area where the day was spent in Musketry Training. C & D Companies doing training under the new scheme for attack.	

S.L.676

From:-
    Officer Commanding,
    15th Batt. Hampshire Regt.

To:-
    Headquarters,
    122nd Infantry Brigade.

Please find enclosed War Diary for the month of May.

G. Douglas Ancrum Major for
_____ Lieut.-Colonel,
Commanding 15th (S.) Batt. Hampshire Regt.

15TH (S) BATTALION,
HAMPSHIRE REGT.

No. ....
Date. 1/6/17.

Army Form C. 2118

WAR DIARY
or
INTELLIGENCE SUMMARY
(Erase heading not required.)

15th Hampshire Regt

Vol 15

13 R
10 she 6

Place	Date	Hour	Summary of Events and Information	Remarks and references to Appendices
TOURNEHEM.	1.5.17		The Battalion carried out the following programme of training in Training Area Extended order drill. Platoon in attack. Company in attack. Recognition, Training out tasks & also General Training. 2nd Lieut Trewitt reported for duty. Weather fine.	
"	2.5.17		A Programme of work was carried out by the Battalion in the Training Area, consisting of the following Extended order Drill followed by Coy. Platoon attack. Musketry. Bombing and Rapid wiring. Also night operations when the Battalion practised an attack in the Training Area. Weather fine	
"	3.5.17		A & B. Companies carried out programme of work in Training area, as follows:- Extended order Drill. Advance Guards & Outposts, Construction of Strong Points, Pushing out Fighting Patrols. and Instruction on Lewis Gun. C. D Companies take Snipers and Transport Firing Practices on A Range in Training Area Weather fine.	Q & D

WAR DIARY
INTELLIGENCE SUMMARY
(Erase heading not required.)

Army Form C. 2118

Instructions regarding War Diaries and Intelligence Summaries are contained in F. S. Regs., Part II. and the Staff Manual respectively. Title Pages will be prepared in manuscript.

Place	Date	Hour	Summary of Events and Information	Remarks and references to Appendices
TOURNEHEM.	4.5.17		The Battalion were engaged in practising a Scheme of Attack. Weather fine.	
"	5.5.17		The programme of work today consisted chiefly of training specialists, work being carried out in Lewis Gun, Bombing, Bayonet fighting and Snipers in Map reading. also drill for living out for digging. A Football Competition was arranged & played amongst H.Q + Companies + Transport. and matches were played between H.Q + A.Coy and Transport v. B.Coy and C v D Companies in which H.Q . B.Coy + D.Coy were victorious (D.Coy beating C.Coy on replay, the first game being a draw). Weather fine.	
"	6.5.17		Battalion attended Church Parade in Company with R.W.Kents after which the G.O.C addressed the Battalion eulogizing on their work in the line. Presenting honours among which, were Military Medal Ribbons to 18024 Sergt Collis and 19025. [Cpl Windebank, for gallantry during the raid by the enemy on the night of the 20th April.	

Army Form C. 2118

WAR DIARY
INTELLIGENCE SUMMARY
(Erase heading not required.)

Place	Date	Hour	Summary of Events and Information	Remarks and references to Appendices
TOURNEHEM	6.5.17	Con'd	The semi final of the Football Competition between H.Q. & B.Coy. (D.Coy having the draw) was played this afternoon in which H.Q. proved victorious by 4-1.	
Do	7.5.17		The programme of work today consisted of practicing a Scheme of attack. The final of the Football Competition was played between H.Q. & D.Coy. & when the whistle sounded time, after a stiff & interesting game, no score had been registered by either team, & after extra time had been played, it was still honours easy with no score. Weather. Fine.	
Do	8.5.17		The Battalion were at work in the training area practising Scheme for continuing pursuit of retreating forces of the enemy. Weather. Fine.	

WAR DIARY

or

INTELLIGENCE SUMMARY

(Erase heading not required.)

Army Form C. 2118

Place	Date	Hour	Summary of Events and Information	Remarks and references to Appendices
TOURNEHEM.	9.5.17		The work of the Battalion today consisted of a scheme for continuing an advance and to prepare a further objective. Weather. Fine.	
"	10.5.17		The Scheme of yesterday, was repeated with certain modifications the scheme practised during the past few days was again repeated. During the afternoon & evening Battalion Sports were held and the final of the Football Competition was replayed in which D Coy were the victors by 1 Goal to Nil. Weather Fine.	
"	11.5.17			
"	12.5.17		The Battalion were engaged in general training, + Companies were allotted the Baths, for which they paraded accordingly. Weather. Fine.	

WAR DIARY

INTELLIGENCE SUMMARY

(Erase heading not required.)

Army Form C. 2118

Place	Date	Hour	Summary of Events and Information	Remarks and references to Appendices
TOURNEHEM	13.5.17		The Battalion attended Church Parade. Weather fine.	
"	14.5.17		The programme of work today was of General Training which included a special lecture of Map reading to all Companies. Weather fine.	
" & LEDERZEELE	15.5.17		The Battalion commenced the march back this morning at 5. a.m. taking the same route to Lederzeele as when coming. Weather fine.	
LEDERZEELE & BEAUVOORDE	16.5.17		Battalion left here this morning taking the route L Menegat - Noordpeene - Buysheene - Brounchove - Ocelave - Cassel - Shenvorde. Weather fine, until evening when there was rain.	
BEAUVOORDE CHIPPEWA CAMP MICMAC CAMP	17.5.17		The Battalion moved off again this morning taking the Route Abeele - Poperinghe - and Reninghelst. H.Q. + A + B Companies staying at Chippewa Camp - C + D Companies going on to Micmac Camp. Weather Drizzly rain until midday, clearing up afterwards.	

WAR DIARY
INTELLIGENCE SUMMARY
(Erase heading not required.)

Army Form C. 2118

Place	Date	Hour	Summary of Events and Information	Remarks and references to Appendices
CHIPPEWA CAMP & MICMAC CAMP	18.5.17		The Battalion supplied various Working Parties, the remainder being engaged on work in Camps. Weather. Fine.	
Do. Do.	19.5.17		Various Working Parties were supplied, remainder engaged in general training & work in Camps. Weather - Fine.	
Do. Do. & ST ELOI SECTOR	20.5.17		The Battalion relieved the 8th Battr W KENT REGT in Reserve, the disposition of Companies being :- H.Q's - Voormezeele. A Coy McGee Trench & Middlesex Lane. B Coy G.H.Q LINE and Ecluse Trench. C Coy + D Coy G.H.Q. LINE. Various Working Parties were supplied. Weather - Fine. Area Quiet.	
ST ELOI SECTOR	21.5.17		Battalion supplied various Working Parties. Area Quiet. Weather. Fine	
Do	22.5.17		Various Working Parties were supplied. 2nd Lieut G.G. Palmer reported for duty. A draft of 14 O.R. joined the Battalion for duty. Area Quiet. Weather. Raining slightly until about 3 o'clock	

Army Form C. 2118

WAR DIARY
or
INTELLIGENCE SUMMARY
(Erase heading not required.)

Instructions regarding War Diaries and Intelligence Summaries are contained in F. S. Regs., Part II. and the Staff Manual respectively. Title Pages will be prepared in manuscript.

Place	Date	Hour	Summary of Events and Information	Remarks and references to Appendices
ST ELOI SECTOR	23.5.17		Battalion supplied various R.E. Working Parties. Area Quiet. Weather Fine.	
Do	24.5.17		Various R.E. Working Parties were supplied near the entrance to Dressing Station at Voormezeele. This morning a shell dropped wounding 19575 L/Cpl Pusey + 27011 L/Cpl Tyler of this Battalion. Area Quiet. Weather Fine	
Do	25.5.17		Battalion supplied various R.E. Working Parties. Area Quiet. Weather Fine	
Do and CHIPPEWA CAMP.	26.5.17		The Battalion was relieved by the 10th QUEENS, and marched back to Chippewa Camp. Working Parties were supplied. Area Quiet. Weather Fine.	
CHIPPEWA CAMP	27.5.17		Various Working Parties were supplied, remainder of Battalion undergoing General Training. Weather Fine.	

1875 Wt. W593/826 1,000,000 4/15 J.B.C. & A. A.D.S.S./Forms/C. 2118.

Army Form C. 2118

WAR DIARY
INTELLIGENCE SUMMARY
(Erase heading not required.)

Instructions regarding War Diaries and Intelligence Summaries are contained in F. S. Regs., Part II. and the Staff Manual respectively. Title Pages will be prepared in manuscript.

Place	Date	Hour	Summary of Events and Information	Remarks and references to Appendices
CHIPPEWA & MICMAC CAMPS	28.5.17		The Battalion supplied various R.E. Working Parties. B. Coy were transferred to Micmac Camp. A draft of **35** O.R. joined the Battalion, which were distributed amongst the Companies. Weather — Fine.	
Do. Do.	29.5.17		The Battalion were allotted the baths for which Companies paraded respectively. Various R.E. Working Parties were supplied. Weather Fine.	
Do. Do.	30.5.17		Various R.E. Working Parties were supplied. Remainder during General Training. Weather Fine.	
Do. Do. & ST. ELOI	31.5.17		The Battalion relieved the 10th Batt. R.W. Kent Regt. in the line, the disposition of Companies being B Coy Right of Sector. A Centre. C Left of Sector. D in Reserve.	

Army Form C. 2118

WAR DIARY
INTELLIGENCE SUMMARY
(Erase heading not required.)

Instructions regarding War Diaries and Intelligence Summaries are contained in F. S. Regs., Part II. and the Staff Manual respectively. Title Pages will be prepared in manuscript.

Place	Date	Hour	Summary of Events and Information	Remarks and references to Appendices
ST ELOI.	31.5.17		The relief was effected without interruption by the enemy. The total casualties for the past 12 months are :— Officers. Killed 15 Wounded <u>19</u> 34. Other Ranks. Killed 117 Missing 73 Wounded <u>536</u> <u>726</u> TOTAL <u>760</u> There was slow continuous fire by our Artillery throughout the day, to which the enemy made no reply. Weather. Fine.	

1875 Wt. W593/826 1,000,000 4/15 J.B.C. & A. A.D.S.S./Forms/C. 2118.

C.L.848.

From:-
    Officer Commanding,
        15th Batt. Hampshire Regt.

To:-
    Headquarters,
        122nd Infantry Brigade.

Please find attached War Diary for the month of June.

                                      G. Douglas Amery
                                                      Major,
                      Commanding 15th Batt. Hampshire Regt.

30/6/17

WAR DIARY
INTELLIGENCE SUMMARY

15 Hampshire Regt
12/4
9.7.14

Place	Date	Hour	Summary of Events and Information	Remarks and references to Appendices
ST ELOI SECTOR	1.6.17		Between 3 A.M and 4.30 A.M. Enemy Artillery was fairly active on our Support line also at Voormezeele - 1.45 p.m he sent over about 15 5.9's in rear of Old French Trench repeating the operation from 4.45 to 5. p.m. During the day our Artillery has been steadily bombarding the enemy front, support and reserve lines, chiefly on Damm Strasse, Pheasant Wood and Craters and a vigorous burst of rapid fire on the night from 6 to 6.10 p.m. It was observed that the enemy wire in front of the Craters is considerably torn. Our trench mortars have shelled the Craters at intervals throughout the day. Two Patrols went out from our trenches for general reconnaissance during the night. Weather. Fine with bright sunshine.	
Do	2.6.17		T M's Enemy shelled our front line opposite Craters during the morning and again at 3 p.m. Our Support + Reserve trenches + Voormezeele were shelled chiefly with 5.9 + 7.7 at short intervals during the day, + our front line (0.21 to 0.27) was also shelled between 3 + 4 p.m. The trench being blown in at 4 places. Our Artillery steadily bombarded the enemy's front line as yesterday + at 9.40 p.m the enemy lines on our right + were heavily bombarded for about 1 hour, when a raid took place from our lines	

Army Form C. 2118

WAR DIARY or INTELLIGENCE SUMMARY
(Erase heading not required.)

Place	Date	Hour	Summary of Events and Information	Remarks and references to Appendices
ST ELOI SECTOR	2.6.17		At 9.40 a.m. a British plane came down in flames North of the Canal, shortly afterwards another landed, under control, near Spoil Bank. This one rose again at 3.30 p.m. Last night, the enemy, in retaliation for the raid on our right, bombarded our front line & communication trenches. He used a number of aërial lights, on no occasion one burst with three red lights & immediately 6 Runi-jars were put over. A Patrol for general reconnaissance went out, who reported that no sign of the enemy's movement could be observed, that his wire is practically demolished, that movement out possible owing to moonlight. We suffered the following casualties:— 26556 Pte Palmer A. (Shell Shock) 27799 Pte Eade C (Shell Shock) 27124 Pte Hallock W.T. (Shell Shock) 31433 Pte Jerom J (Wounded) 27183 L/Cpl King (Wounded) remained at duty. 26908 Pte Adams A. + 20426 Pte Pearce (Wounded) Weather Fine.	
Do.	3.6.17		Enemy artillery has been active shelling chiefly our reserve & support lines. Also Voormezeele & area further back. Our artillery was again active steadily bombarding enemy front support & reserve lines, increasing to a vigorous bombardment at 11.20 a.m. + 3 p.m.	

WAR DIARY
~~INTELLIGENCE SUMMARY~~
(Erase heading not required.)

Army Form C. 2118

Place	Date	Hour	Summary of Events and Information	Remarks and references to Appendices
ST ELOI SECTOR	3.6.17		Nothing about half an hour in each case 11.30 a.m. 11.45 a.m. our Stokes Guns were dropping shells on Craters 2.3.4 & 5. Considerable aerial activity on both sides, but no encounters have been seen. 2 Patrols of one officer + 15 O.R. and 1 officer + 14 O.R. went out from our trenches to patrol & if possible penetrate enemy lines, but owing to enemy Gas shells were obliged to return, unsuccessful. A covering Patrol taken two other Reconnoitring Patrols went out, but could been no movement in enemy lines. Casualties:— 28011 Pte Draper (Killed) 25954 L/Cpl Corney 28000 Pte Hocking 31580 Pte Tidridge B. (Wounded)	
Do	4.6.17	12 midnight Between / and 2 a.m.	the enemy sent over Gas Lachrimatory Shells into our Front + support lines, necessitating the wearing of Gas respirators, & his artillery has been fairly active throughout the day chiefly shelling our support + communication trenches also on Voormezeele. Our Artillery has been steadily bombarding the enemy's Front, support and	

WAR DIARY
INTELLIGENCE SUMMARY

Army Form C. 2118

Place	Date	Hour	Summary of Events and Information	Remarks and references to Appendices
ST ELOI SECTOR	4.6.17		Cont'd/ Reserve lines, Damm Strasse and Pheasant Wood. Our light medium heavy T.M's bombarding enemy front line between 1.50 & 2.45 pm. Three Patrols left our trenches to reconnoitre enemy's wire, which was found to be very weak, & in places non existent. The noval standing Patrol reported that no enemy movement could be seen or heard. Casualties:- 18450 Pte Clements. 28012 Pte Slomp. N. 24766 Pte S.H.W. 27520 Sergt Bennett 22895 Pte Cheesman. D. 20771 Bushnell. W. 24876 Payne G.W. & 18250 Gunman J. Gassed. 17994 L/Cpl. Lewis R. Wounded. Weather - Fine.	4
Do and MIDDLE CAMP WEST (M 6.B.9.5)	5.6.17		Enemy Artillery had been active again today:- 2.30 to 5 a.m. he sent over about 8 7.7 c.m on the right of old French Trench, including two direct hits on the R.A.P.- VOORMEZEELE and Area behind were also shelled at intervals during the day. Our Artillery has been steadily bombarding enemy lines as yesterday, The Battalion were relieved by the West (Riding) where remainder of the day was spent in cleaning up and marched to Middle Camp. Weather Fine, and Hot.	

Army Form C. 2118

WAR DIARY
INTELLIGENCE SUMMARY
(Erase heading not required.)

Instructions regarding War Diaries and Intelligence Summaries are contained in F. S. Regs., Part II. and the Staff Manual respectively. Title Pages will be prepared in manuscript.

Place	Date	Hour	Summary of Events and Information	Remarks and references to Appendices
MIDDLE CAMP WEST.	5.6.17		Casualties :— 2nd Lieut P. J. Collier Gassed — 26886 Pte Court H. 15734 Pte Payne H. Pte Stuck Gassed — 16325 Pte Guelff. W. 4494 Pte Brook E. 20719 L/Cpl Searle - Wounded.	
Do & POSITION OF ASSEMBLY FOR ATTACK. (Old French Trench)	6.6.17		The Battalion details and reinforcements marched to Divisional Reinforcement Camp, Reninghelst, and at 8.50 p.m. The Battalion marched to position of assembly which was accomplished without opposition from the enemy + after arrival no difficulty arose in lying down in the open between Old French Locality Trenches, when the enemy's barrage had previously been fairly consistently watched + which was allowed for. A draft of 13. O.R. joined the Battalion for duty.	
	7.6.17	12.10 a.m.	We had however a few casualties including 2nd Lieut M Moore + 2nd Lieut Daniels both wounded	
		At zero hour (3.10 a.m.)	we blew a large mine under the enemy's craters at St Eloi at the same time our Artillery opened barrage, when the 123rd Brigade commenced attacking — Two hours later we moved up in Artillery formation to the DAMMSTRASSE + upon arrival there we deployed into position ready for the attack. Our own barrage	

WAR DIARY
or
INTELLIGENCE SUMMARY
(Erase heading not required.)

Army Form C. 2118

Place	Date	Hour	Summary of Events and Information	Remarks and references to Appendices
DAGSTRASSE	7.6.17		was excellent on the right but very ragged on the left and centre. At this point we lost Lieut Newman (wounded in leg)	
		6.50 A.M.	We moved forward on our objective. Many casualties were caused by the guns remaining on the second objective on the left, + it was not until the Artillery were informed, that it was finally occupied, after this barrage moved forward. Shortly after reaching final objective Capt. Gorman 2nd Lieut Cope and 2nd Lieut Wright were wounded	
		9.10 A.M.	It was observed that enemy were moving in the valley beyond Observn Row and at 10.15 a.m. 500 men were rushed over the ridge just behind to join them. These were received with pretty heavy Lewis Gun fire, and severe casualties were caused. From this period onwards, various attempts to make a local counter attack on Denys Wood were made; these took place at 10 am and 3 and 7 pm. None of the attacks were in any degree successful and the one at 3 pm was unexpectedly met by our own attack carried out by the 24th Division. Prior to these attacks we were subjected to intense	

WAR DIARY
INTELLIGENCE SUMMARY.
(Erase heading not required.)

Army Form C. 2118.

Place	Date	Hour	Summary of Events and Information	Remarks and references to Appendices
OBSCURE SUPPORT	8/6/17		bombardments, which died away when our Artillery opened fire. Our casualties were not heavy, A Coy suffering most severely + 2nd Lieut Rhepu O/C Coy was killed. We occupied OBSCURE SUPPORT until 3.15 am the 8th when we were relieved by a unit of the 73rd Brigade then came back to Old French Trench + remained there, being joined by the Battalion reinforcements in the evening. List of Casualties on Page 14.15.16.	
OLD FRENCH TRENCH	9/6/17		The enemy put over a few shells in this area, but doing no damage, otherwise area quiet. A draft of 29 O.R. joined this Battalion 2nd Lieut Gosworth reported for duty.	
D.	10/6/17		Except for occasional shells dropping in the vicinity this area was quiet until 10.25 p.m when there was intense bombardment by our Artillery, lasting about an hour during which the Battalion were 'standing to' "C" Coy were attached for working parties to R.E. Coy at Dickebusch.	

WAR DIARY
INTELLIGENCE SUMMARY.
(Erase heading not required.)

Army Form C. 2118.

Place	Date	Hour	Summary of Events and Information	Remarks and references to Appendices
OLD FRENCH TRENCH	11.6.17.		With the exception of a few shells falling in the neighbourhood the area was quiet. Weather fine.	
Do & SUPPORT LINE	12.6.17		Battalion moved up the line in Support. Disposition of Companies being H.Q's in Car Alley, A. Coy Car Road. B & D Coys Old Boot Trench, — digging and renovating trenches & making dugouts being carried on	
Do	13.6.17		There was intermittent shelling of our lines by the enemy during the day. The work of digging trenches & making dugouts was carried on. We had Casualties in 18301 Pte Wright. C. Died of wounds. 16819 L/Cpl Pearce. J. and 31803. L/Cpl Morris both wounded.	
Do	14.6.17		The work of consolidating our position was carried on. At 7.30 p.m two Battalions on our left front made an attack successfully capturing & holding their objective. Casualties:- 17660. Cpl Jago J. 17385. Pte Fox. C. 26406. Pte Millard. W. } Awarded 328 L. R.E. 35171. — Peckham E. 21083. Pte Quenlett F. }	

WAR DIARY
INTELLIGENCE SUMMARY
(Erase heading not required.)

Army Form C. 2118.

Place	Date	Hour	Summary of Events and Information	Remarks and references to Appendices
	15.6.17		Enemy shelled our trenches at intervals during the day & at 7.30 p.m. heavily at which time he made a counter attack on the position gained by this Battalion on our left front, yesterday, but was driven back.	
WHITE CHATEAU.	16.6.17		The Battalion (reporting C.O. who are still shelled to 2P8 & (0) R.E.) relieved the 12th Batt. K.R.R. in the line, the disposition of Companies being H.Q. - WHITE CHATEAU. A C.O. OPAL RESERVE (2 Platoons) and 2 Platoons OLIVE TRENCH, B C.O. OLIVE TRENCH. D C.O. OPTIC TRENCH.	
		17 6.17	At 10.20 p.m. the enemy put a barrage on Opal Reserve & Optic Trench & further back along Oblong Alley as far as White Chateau which came in for the winds shelling. At 10.30 p.m. the S.O.S. was sent up from our front line, which was replied from White Chateau. Our own barrage was put down very quickly and the enemy, a few of whom left their trenches, were dispersed by that own Lewis Gun fire. Casualties 18849. Pte Johnstone. J.	

Army Form C. 2118.

WAR DIARY
or
INTELLIGENCE SUMMARY.
(Erase heading not required.)

Instructions regarding War Diaries and Intelligence Summaries are contained in F. S. Regs., Part II. and the Staff Manual respectively. Title pages will be prepared in manuscript.

Place	Date	Hour	Summary of Events and Information	Remarks and references to Appendices
WHITE CHATEAU	17/6/17		There has been intermittent shelling of our front support line throughout the day. Hostile Chateau came in for heavy shelling at 11.20 a.m. when a heavy shell exploded in a small portion. Enemy planes were early active today. Two of them made repeated visits. They remained long along our lines at intervals between 6 a.m. and 12 noon opening fire along the trench with their Machine Guns. During the three visits our position was incidently shelled with whizzbang & shrapnel from 3.55 G.S. Our heavy artillery has been firing short, quite a number of shells falling within 30 yards of our line. They are presumably shelling Dolbekie. We suffered the following casualties:- 18747 Sergt. Sams.W. 26876. Sergt. Brooks.R. and 17341. Drummer Jelmingham were killed the following were wounded:- 27505. Pte. Lilley F. 28006 R/S Pte Allen 26 June Pte Clark.T.W. 26692. Pte Hornibrow 235024 Pte Trunch. R. 18009 Pte Bollom.T. and 2nd Lieut Donaldson who was also wounded.	
Do	18.6.17		Enemy artillery was fairly quiet last night. Opal Reserve being shelled at intervals. During the day he has apparently been registering on the Battalion front with 5.9s 4.2 & some field Guns, the former were put on the Communication	

WAR DIARY
INTELLIGENCE SUMMARY
(Erase heading not required.)

Army Form C. 2118.

Place	Date	Hour	Summary of Events and Information	Remarks and references to Appendices
Trenches & later, on Front Line	18.6.17		Chateau (B.H.Q) from 7.30 am to 12.30 pm Front Line which was evacuated the enemy was making a strong point and also an O.P. was razed to the ground by our artillery. Hostile aircraft were again active from 4.30 this morning flying very low, one or more were spotting for 5.9 Battery which during the whole shelling this morning firing very light. In addition they fired into our trenches. Our casualties were:- 25774 Sergt Brookes W. 18009 Pte Buck R. 28004 Pte Trewlove G. wounded and the following attached 6.228 Coy R.E. 27726 L.Cpl Benetto 24710. Pte Simpson 8. Killed and 27140. Pte Huggins I. and 24745. Pte Reid W. wounded.	
	19.6.17		Enemy artillery has been considerably less active today. The chief feature being a bombardment of our support trenches + more especially our communication trenches the latter being shelled with 4.2'S, Whizzbangs + H.E. Shrapnel. While Chateau was shelled occasionally Retaliation by our guns but Field Trench Heavy has been most effective.	

WAR DIARY
INTELLIGENCE SUMMARY
(Erase heading not required.)

Army Form C. 2118.

Place	Date	Hour	Summary of Events and Information	Remarks and references to Appendices

	19.6.17		Cont/ The usual hostile aeroplane flew low over our Sector between 5.30 & 6.30 a.m. firing into our support line several times, but was driven off by some very accurate shooting from one of our Field guns which nearly hit him. A little later some of our own machines put in an appearance, with the result that during the rest of the day there was a marked decrease in the number of machines able to approach our positions closely enough for effective observation.	
Bivouac Camp N5A.9.8. Gordon Farm	20.6.17		During the night the Battalion were relieved by the 23rd Batt. MIDDLESEX REGT and marched back to Bivouacs at N.5A.9.8. Casualties:- 235022 Pte. Saunders R. 24657. Pte. Morris A. 27220. Pte. Rogers W. 29658. Pte. Horne R. wounded. Working Parties were supplied, remainder having a General clean up.	
D.	21.6.17 to 26.6.17		Various Working Parties were supplied and general training of the Battalion being carried out. During the afternoon of the 26th Battalion moved to another Camp in tents at C.6.4. (MILLEKRUISSE) 25163 Pte Metcalf R. wounded. 9248. Pte Jones M. wounded.	

N 2 C. C.4. (MILLEKRUISSE)

WAR DIARY

INTELLIGENCE SUMMARY.

Army Form C. 2118.

Place	Date	Hour	Summary of Events and Information	Remarks and references to Appendices
N.2.C.6.4. (MILLEKRUSSE)	26.6.17 to 30.6.17		Various R.E. Working Parties were supplied daily, and general training of the Battalion carried out. On the 27th we suffered the following casualties in one of our Working Parties sent out. 31607 Pte Gilbert. W. Killed. 20521. Pte Anell. E. Died of wounds. 17980 Pte Pearson J. Wounded. 33086. Pte Patten. A. Wounded.	

Army Form C. 2118.

WAR DIARY
or
INTELLIGENCE SUMMARY
(Erase heading not required.)

Summary of Events and Information

List of Casualties incurred on 7th June 1917.

Officers - Killed - 2nd Lieut. W. G. Kopp
And of Wounds - 2nd Lieut W. G. Wright
Officers Wounded - Capt. D. T. Gorman   Capt. J. Hudson R.A.M.C.   Lieut. C.C. Newman   2nd Lieut. J.E. Coope   2nd Lieut. M.S. Moore   2nd Lieut. J.A. O'Daniels.

KILLED

25340 L/Cpt New E	16798 Pte Bailey J.C.	27023 L/Cpl McKenzie G	281804 Pte Kladows G
14439 Pte Borton G	28006 " Bayliss R	28015 Pte Babinett R	18672 Sgt Grant W
14695 " Cooper G	27072 " Lidiard G	18333 " Hill A	12762 Pte Hill S
26973 " Lee R	21000 " Newnham F	25097 " Pink E	
18008 " Leal W	19237 " Simms A	23460 " Longe J	MISSING
27030 " Shaw H	21084 " Sandeman J	23247 " Burch W	27221 Pte Kemp F
25324 " Cooper F	27194 " Roberts G	25139 " Eves T	27048 " Hymas
27110 " Hoskins C	27782 L/Cpl Woodford W.H	21561 " O'Brien L	26995 " Hinge J
19176 " Turner G	27126 Pte Rundell G	29211 " Copeland	
26890 " Tee W G	20729 " Halen E	28023 " Newton A.T.	
27031 " Barnett J	3463 " Maples J	26909 " Blake J	
	26924 Sgt Inslow B	26977 " Pike J	

Army Form C. 2118.

WAR DIARY
or
INTELLIGENCE SUMMARY.
(Erase heading not required.)

Instructions regarding War Diaries and Intelligence Summaries are contained in F. S. Regs., Part II. and the Staff Manual respectively. Title pages will be prepared in manuscript.

Place	Date	Hour	Summary of Events and Information	Remarks and references to Appendices
			WOUNDED 7th June, 1917.	

17996	Sergt Murdoch S	25257	Pte Thomas F	12979	Pte Osbourne W J
25813	L/Cpl Corbett F	252256	" Vise A	33087	" Padley J F
8660	" Hall P	22348	" Dalley C	27075	" Palmer E
27499	" Johnson G	26985	" Willmott G.J	23350	" Shotman P V
25131	Pte Barton F	17416	" Shadwick G.G	20429	" Shearns E M R
27167	" Cook W	8083	C.S.M. Pratt W	25051	" Shees G
18028	" Coleman J	19115	Sergt Longnight L	27010	" Tibble F L
25343	" Creamer J	27176	" Willie H L	18337	Taylor W J
31627	" Dove S	26275	1 Cpl Lockyer T	20283	Johns D
27162	" Gilbert J	28884	" Summerys W N	20941	Read H J
17303	" Grummitt C	31595	" Brown E C	27998	Rowing R
31626	" Hampton S	27133	" Blanning J	10977	Barker
20418	" Hatch A	31997	Pte Brady I	27042	Polford A
18287	" Harris I	34792	" Bramble E J	18491	Lyles T H
9649	" Innes F	30033	" Deacon B	20674	L/Sergt Dixon R G
20739	" Jackman G	27161	" Dryden J F	16801	A/Sergt Skeene W.H
27115	" Mitchell G	30945	" Lyles R	21781	Cpl Gatland E
17269	" Richardson B	28002	" Wright A	27013	" Whittle F.T
29816	" Smith T	17371	" Kelley W	18025	" Windowsick G (Shell Shock)
26981	" Standridge R			27022	L/Cpl Lees R.N

WAR DIARY
INTELLIGENCE SUMMARY.
(Erase heading not required.)

Army Form C. 2118.

Place	Date	Hour	Summary of Events and Information				Remarks and references to Appendices
			7th June 1917				
			WOUNDED				
			27152	Pte Beer R	17207	Pte Lunford E	Pte Court
			31737	" Blunn J	27789	" Button	" Heath R
			3592	" Barrow F	33340	" Morgan F.R	" Brick A
			18864	" Coe R.J	26271	Corpl Faulkner S	" Carter K.S
			21159	" Campbell G	21054	" Mordy C	" Eveleigh W
			26454	" Collins T.W	27784	" Dunne N.J	
			18667	" Dicks J	27497	L/Cpl McKenzie M	
			27077	" Smith S	27237	" Millard W	
			27790	" Dunning C	27496	" Mitchell A	
			25574	" Fry E	19417	" Heath T	
			27138	" Gladstone E	12717	Pte Avery A	
			16283	" Holloway R.J	27066	" Budge A	
			9070	L/Cpl Hickman W	27173	" Brenton J	
			17975	Pte Murphy A	31616	" Bright P	
			27095	" Nicks W.H	7751	" Barker E	
			10565	" Rowland A	28016	" Broughton J	
			14095	" Smith C	20577	" Collins H	
			27516	" Tiller G	28014	" Coombs H	
			20751	" Underdown T	26914	" Davey J	
			27533	" Vincent J	27218	" Gibbs E.G	
			27033	" Wesley R	26765	" Hood H	
			16422	" Wheelwright C	19394	" Hartnell A	
			20453	" Ford A.C	21619	" Harding V	
			27050	" Lambert F.T	25044	" Hutchinson V	
					28010	Pte Jeans J	27191
					28008	" Jennard W	31629
					22979	" Later W	31620
					26960	" Morgan R	27067
					27029	" Owens P	20435
					33305	" Pollard S	
					20203	" Reed W	
					19433	" Skene A	
					28017	" Salisbury C	
					12611	" Turner E	
					100604	" Wheeler C	
					28012	" Dunn P.C	
					26419	" Redding W	
					24209	" Somers W	
					19100	" Scott P	
					21026	" Wiles A.C	
					27085	" Salley H	
					3/4033	" Finlay J.F	
					26979	" Richards F	
					10264	" Connie J	
					25298	" Tiegenna T	
					26950	" Hunt B	
					27164	" Bray F	

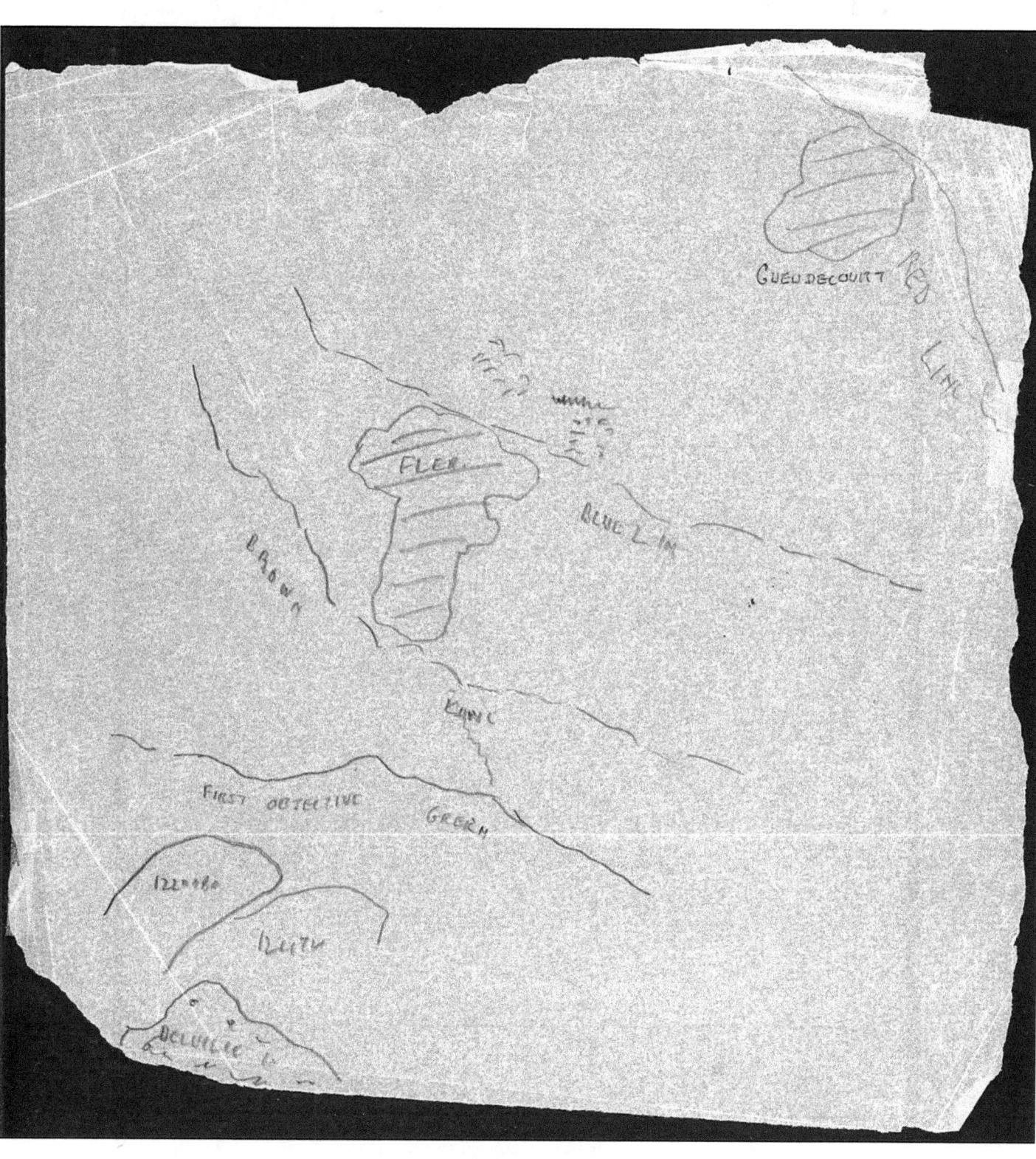

"C" Form.
MESSAGES AND SIGNALS.

Army Form C. 2123.
(In books of 100.)
No. of Message ....

Prefix SM	Code AE	Words 10	Received From ES29 By Mackey	Sent or sent out At .... m. To .... By	Office Stamp.

Charges to collect

Service Instructions. FS29

Handed in at Bow Office 1.25 a.m. Received 1.45 a.m.

TO EV13 (Bell)

*Sender's Number	Day of Month	In reply to Number	A A A
P732	10th		

Relief Complete aaa

FROM PLACE & TIME Bow 1.25 a.m.

* This line should be erased if not required.

"O" Form.
MESSAGES AND SIGNALS.

Army Form C. 2123.
(In books of 100.)
No. of Message.........

Prefix........ Code........ Words........
Charges to collect
Service Instructions.

Received From EN77 By Mackay

Sent, or sent out At........ m. To........ By........

Office Stamp.
ZEB - 9.IV.17
TELEGRAPHS

Handed in at EN77 Hamlet .... Office 10.49 p.m. Received 10.52 p.m.

TO EN13 (Bell)

*Sender's Number	Day of Month	In reply to Number	A A A
375M	7th		

BOO No 99 compleat with
aaa time 10.15PM aaa

FROM
PLACE & TIME EN77 (Hamlet)

*This line should be erased if not required.

"O" Form.
MESSAGES AND SIGNALS.

Army Form C. 2123.
(In books of 100.)
No. of Message

Prefix	Code	Words	Received From	Sent, or sent out	Office Stamp.
Charges to collect	£ s. d.		By	At .... m	
Service Instructions.				To .... By	

Handed in at .... Office .... m. Received .... m.

TO

*Sender's Number	Day of Month	In reply to Number	A A A
	10		

FROM
PLACE & TIME

* This line should be erased if not required.

"A" Form.
MESSAGES AND SIGNALS.

No. of Message 8

Prefix	Code	m.	Words	Charge	This message is on a/c of:	Recd. at	m.
Office of Origin and Service Instructions.			Sent			Date	
			At	m	Service.	From	
			To				
			By		(Signature of "Franking Officer.")	By	

TO ~~H J I W G~~

Sender's Number.	Day of Month.	In reply to Number.	AAA
BN 2	10		

| O.O | 10# | complied with | by |
| left | Bn | | |

From
Place 122 Inf Bde
Time

The above may be forwarded as now corrected. (Z)

WAR DIARY
INTELLIGENCE SUMMARY

Army Form C. 2118.

Place	Date	Hour	Summary of Events and Information	Remarks and references to Appendices
N.2.C.6.4. (MILLEKRUISSE)	1.7.17		Various R.E. Working Parties were supplied and the Battalion did General Training in this area, but not enough was done in this Camp, otherwise, Area quiet. At 10.30 p.m. the Enemy sent over a few shells	M. Davis
Do	2.7.17 3.7.17		Various R.E. Working Parties were supplied and the Battalion did General Training.	
Do	4.7.17		Do. At 9.20 a.m. this morning His Majesty King George V passed this Camp, going in direction of firing line.	
Do	5.7.17		Various R.E. Working Parties were supplied and the Battalion did General training.	
Do	6.7.17		Do. A draft of 129. O.R. joined the Battalion this day. 2nd Lieut P. Warren and 2nd Lieut H.G. Savage also reported for duty.	

WAR DIARY

INTELLIGENCE SUMMARY.

Army Form C. 2118.

Place	Date	Hour	Summary of Events and Information	Remarks and references to Appendices
N.2.C.6.4. (MILLEKRUISSE)	7.7.17		Various R.E. Working Parties were supplied and general training carried out. We supplied the following casualties in one of R.E. Work Parties sent out today. 2nd Lieut H Warren. 9950 L/Cpl Taylor W.H and 20422 Pte Knight W. killed and 27180 L/Cpl Brandon 28000 Pte Gaynor. 33088 Pte Lilly and 27155 L/Cpl Russell were wounded	
Do	8.7.17 9.7.17		Various R.E. Working Parties were supplied and general training done	
Do	10.7.17		Do Do 10958. Pte Roofs and 11904 Pte G. Taylor were wounded while on working party	
Do & 27 R 34 A 5.9 (SCHAXKEN)	11.7.17		R.E. Working Parties were supplied. The Battalion moved to Billets at Schaeken. H.Q being at R.34 A 5. 9. A draft of 113. O.R joined the Battalion today	
Do	12.7.17		The Battalion spent the day in General Training	

WAR DIARY
INTELLIGENCE SUMMARY.
(Erase heading not required.)

Army Form C. 2118.

Place	Date	Hour	Summary of Events and Information	Remarks and references to Appendices
27 R 34 A.5.9 (SCHAYKEN)	13.7.17		The Battalion spent the morning in General training and in the afternoon were inspected by the Divisional Commander accompanied by the Brigade Commander & after the inspection the Div Commander addressed the Battalion expressing his pleasure for but work taken on the recent offensive, after which he presented honours to various officers & men for gallantry in the recent operations.	
Do	14.7.17		The Battalion did General Training Specialists having separate classes of instruction	
Do	15.7.17		After Church Parade this morning, the Battalion spent the day in recreation.	
Do	16.7.17		General Training and Classes of Instruction for Specialists. A draft of 20 O.R joined the Battalion. 2nd Lieut H M Tollemache and 2nd Lieut R E Markham reported for duty with the Battalion.	

Army Form C. 2118.

WAR DIARY
INTELLIGENCE SUMMARY.
(Erase heading not required.)

Instructions regarding War Diaries and Intelligence
Summaries are contained in F. S. Regs., Part II.
and the Staff Manual respectively. Title pages
will be prepared in manuscript.

Place	Date	Hour	Summary of Events and Information	Remarks and references to Appendices
27R.34.A.5.9. (SCHAXKEN)	17.7.17		General training and Special classes for specialists was carried out.	
Do	18.7.17		General training until 10.30 a.m. the remainder of the day being given up to the Battalion Sports which proved a great success, and to which the G.O.C. Brigade paid a visit	
Do	19.7.17 20.7.17 21.7.17		The Battalion were occupied in the training of Specialists and General training	
Do	22.7.17		The Battalion attended Church Parade this morning, after which the C.O. presented Divisional Cards to various men of the Battalion for gallantry in the recent operations	
Do & MURRUMBIGEE CAMP.	23.7.17		The Battalion marched to Murrumbidgee Camp	

Army Form C. 2118.

WAR DIARY
of
INTELLIGENCE SUMMARY.
(Erase heading not required.)

Instructions regarding War Diaries and Intelligence Summaries are contained in F.S. Regs., Part II. and the Staff Manual respectively. Title pages will be prepared in manuscript.

Place	Date	Hour	Summary of Events and Information	Remarks and references to Appendices
MORRUMBIDGEE ZH & CAMP P & O TRENCH BOIS CONFLUENT	24.7.17		The Battalion relieved the 7th Batt. London Regt. in reserve. Reinforcements and details marching to Brigade Reinforcement Camp at WOOD CAMP. 27510 Pte Fanner was killed and 27004 L/Cpl Magill + 9584 L/Cpl Jacobs were wounded.	
Do. Do. 25.7.17	25.7.17		Various R.E. Working Parties were supplied, the first 5 of which, ordered for the 517th Co R.E. were not met + in consequence returned, they were eventually ordered to report to 228 C. R.E. Area quiet. Weather Fine.	
Do.	26.7.17		Various R.E. Working Parties were supplied. Area quiet. Weather, raining during morning until noon clearing later.	
Do.	27.7.17		The enemy artillery were inactive during today until 8 p.m. when he heavily bombarded our line, which lasted until 10 p.m. We supplied various R.E. Working Parties. There were 10 casualties. 2 k. 8 w. Weather, Fine.	

Army Form C. 2118.

WAR DIARY
INTELLIGENCE SUMMARY.
(Erase heading not required.)

Instructions regarding War Diaries and Intelligence Summaries are contained in F.S. Regs., Part II. and the Staff Manual respectively. Title pages will be prepared in manuscript.

Place	Date	Hour	Summary of Events and Information	Remarks and references to Appendices
BOIS CONFLUENT P&O TRENCH	28.7.17		The enemy bombarded our trenches with mustard gas shells during the night 28th-29th between midnight & 2.30 am. The shells were of H.2 & 5.9 calibre. Mustard oil gas had not been known to be used very often in shells of this size. It was duly reported to Brigade. No casualties were reported as result of this gas. Various R.E. Working parties were supplied. Weather	
Do Do	29.7.17		Enemy artillery were a little more active today ending our 4.2 and 5.9 at intervals during the day. We supplied Various R.E. Working Parties. Weather fine	
Do Do	30.7.17		Enemy Artillery were inactive until 12 noon when they opened a vigorous bombardment of our trenches with 4.2 & 5.9. Shrapnel which lasted until 2.30 pm	

Army Form C. 2118.

WAR DIARY
or
INTELLIGENCE SUMMARY.
(Erase heading not required.)

Place	Date	Hour	Summary of Events and Information	Remarks and references to Appendices
Ramp? Grounds BOIS CONFLUENT	31.7.17		Zero Day for the attack on HOLLEBEKE. At 3.50 a.m. (zero hour) the 122nd Inf. Brigade made an attack on a two battalion front the final objective extending from FORÊT FARM on the right to the KLEIN ZILLEBEKE ROAD on the left. The 18th K.R.R's on the right, the 11th Bn. R.W.K. on the left. Each battalion attacked on a two Coy. front each Coy. being on a four platoon front. The attack was carried out in two waves three objectives being taken (Red, Blue and Green lines) and was in every successful. The only serious opposition met with being at FORÊT FARM by which the right Coy. was held up for several hours by M.G. fire. This was afterwards taken by the same Bn. In the evening of the same day the position of the 15th Bn. Hants. Regt. during the attack was as follows: three Companies in BOIS CONFLUENT one Coy (B) in LOCK HOUSE TUNNELS SPOIL BANK. Bn. H.Q. BOIS CONFLUENT. At 10 a.m. the three Coys in BOIS CONFLUENT moved up to a position between EIK HOF F^m and OAK DUMP and C.H.Q. moved to SPOIL BANK. At 11 p.m. A and D Coys were moved up again to a support position Bn. H.Q. at BOIS CONFLUENT was shelled with gas from 2 a.m. in morning. Weather very wet after 4 p.m.	

WAR DIARY
or
INTELLIGENCE SUMMARY.
(Erase heading not required.)

Army Form C. 2118.

Place	Date	Hour	Summary of Events and Information	Remarks and references to Appendices
Loos Huyse Cenard	31/1/17		The number of casualties for the day in the front line trenches being caused by a gun shell.	

May-Darmod
Lieut.—Colonel.
Commanding 15th (S.) Batt. Hampshire Regt.

Army Form C. 2118.

WAR DIARY
INTELLIGENCE SUMMARY.
(Erase heading not required.)

Instructions regarding War Diaries and Intelligence Summaries are contained in F. S. Regs., Part II. and the Staff Manual respectively. Title pages will be prepared in manuscript.

Page 1.

Place	Date	Hour	Summary of Events and Information	Remarks and references to Appendices
LOCK HOUSE CELLARS	Aug 1st 1917		Battalion remained in support, H.Q. at LOCK HOUSE CELLARS, A + D Coys at OBLIQUE ROW + OPTIC TRENCH C, at OAK SUPPORT B. SPOIL BANK. The enemy shelled our positions intermittently otherwise the day was uneventful. Rain fell incessantly + conditions were extraordinarily bad, the men being in many cases up to their waists in mud + water. Casualties O.R. 8 killed 30 Wounded	
	2/8/17		Battalion remains in support. Artillery not quite so active. Rain continues to fall + conditions are getting worse, the trenches are full of water + most of the men have been moved to shell holes Casualties Lt. S.A.C. PEARSE & 2/Lt A.J. ADAMS wounded. O.R. one wounded	
	3/8/17		Battalion remains in support. had weather continues. The day passed uneventfully no particular hostile activity of any kind being apparent. At night we relieved the 11. R.W. KENTS in the line, two companies in front line, the remainder of the Battalion being disposed in the OAK HOUSE TUNNELS + OAK SUPPORT. relief being complete at 2.0 AM	

WAR DIARY or INTELLIGENCE SUMMARY

Army Form C. 2118.

Place	Date	Hour	Summary of Events and Information	Remarks and references to Appendices
	3/8/17		Casualties O.R. one wounded	
Iron Bridge Tunnels	4/8/17		Another uneventful day until about 10.0 P.M. when hostile shelling started on all areas of our front. It continued almost incessantly throughout the night right up to the time the barrage started for the attack which was made on the morning of the 5th. 2nd Lt. M.S.S. Moore & a draft of 29 O.R. reported for duty at WOOD CAMP. Weather improving. Casualties O.R. 11 wounded	

WAR DIARY
INTELLIGENCE SUMMARY

Army Form C. 2118.

Place	Date	Hour	Summary of Events and Information	Remarks and references to Appendices
IRON BRIDGE TUNNELS	5/8/17	4.0 am	At 4.0 am in a heavy mist the enemy attempted to retake HOLLEBEKE. He succeeded in getting into FORRET FARM, & tried to take HOLLEBEKE. This occurring round the rear as well as round the front. Capt. J.P. FOWLER slightly withdrew his company from HOLLEBEKE & cut off a small party who had got behind him. The left side of this party was taken prisoner except 1 Sergeant + 15 men, held firm. The whole of this post was afterwards seen dead who returned + one man who was afterwards seen dead. Very little information reaching Batt. H.Q. Major G.D. AMERY + 2nd/Lt S. LASSENBY went forward to clear up the situation, on further information the 2 companies who had previously been in reserve, were sent forward in support to OPAL RESERVE the C.O. proceeded to OPTIC TRENCH, at that moment a message arrived from Capt. J.P. FOWLER giving his dispositions an immediate counter-attack under cover of the mist was ordered. Major G.D. AMERY having become a casualty Capt. C.C. OXBORROW'S Coy. advanced with some men of the 12th East Surrey Regt. + eventually passed to re-enter HOLLEBEKE. One platoon from the reserve company was detailed to attack FORRET FARM with the assistance of some men of the 12th E.S. Regt. In addition a Company was ordered to do the same thing, but came up on Epine Thing, in the meantime while the The Village + FORRET FARM were cleaned + 17 prisoners taken. H.Q. 12th E. Surrey Regt. HQ. rocked personally achieving above orders were being put into effect by means of Maj. R. PENNELL personally the above given the C.O. ordered to the 12th E Surrey Rgt HQ rocked for a plans rate of fire for 1/4 of an hour then rapid for same period followed again by a further burst of fire which was carried out. Clear line concealed with the fortuitously attack	

Place	Date	Hour	Summary of Events and Information	Remarks and references to Appendices
IRON BRIDGE TUNNELS			ON HOLLEBEKE. On arrival at FORRET FARM a STAFFORD officer was reorganising some of the 15th Batt HANTS Regt he handed over the command to 2/Lt P.E. SHIELDS & the HANTS & SURREYS set off for FORRET FARM taking 13 prisoners. E Company of the STAFFORDS were brought up at 2/Lt P.E. SHIELDS' request & placed by in support 200 yds in rear, but were not required. NOTE. From later information it appears that in addition to the enemy divisions opposing us some 100 "STURMTRUPPEN" specially selected, in then phyique & intelligence took part in the attack, which were carried out in a large scale but in spite of this, the fact that our men were wet through & tired out, the enemy gained no advantage whatever & had heavy casualties. The officer taken prisoner was 2/Lt R.E. Martin. The Lt/Lion he had, but in The Lin.	
		DUSK	Our forward positions were reinforced by Y Company	
		7.30 P.M	Enemy were observed massing for another attack & at 8.30 P.M they commenced crawling towards our line, but were completely dispersed by M.G, rifle fire & a well timed barrage, on lines previously noted.	
O.5.c.7.9		NIGHT	Batt H.Q. move to a set in the CANAL BANK at O.5.c.7.9. These H.Q. had previously been occupied by 12th E. Surreys.	

WAR DIARY or INTELLIGENCE SUMMARY

Army Form C. 2118

Place	Date	Hour	Summary of Events and Information	Remarks and references to Appendices
O.5.c.7.9.	5/8/17		Casualties. 2/Lt H.J. SHERYER died of wounds. Maj G.D. AMERY wounded. 2/Lt R.E. MARTIN missing believed P.of.W. O.R. 10 killed, 10 wounded, 1 died of wounds, 7 missing believed P.of.W.	
	6/8/17	3.15 am	Enemy put a barrage on our forward posts which did not however materialise into any attack.	
		Evening	"Z" Coy formed a platoon of about 60 men from each Battalion in the Brigade came up from WOOD CAMP & two platoons in support at OPPIE TRENCH, OBLIQUE ROW, WHITE CHATEAU & OAK SUPPORT	
			Weather Morning FAIR. afternoon RAIN. Casualties 2/Lt G.G. PALMER } wounded. O.R. 10 wounded 2/Lt J.L. SPENCER }	
	7/8/17	9.15 pm	Exceptionally quiet all day until 9.15 pm. Enemy started heavy bombardment on the left from just North of the Canal. Our guns opened in retaliation, & the enemy immediately put up his reddish red light (S.O.S) which had the effect of checking	

WAR DIARY
or
INTELLIGENCE SUMMARY

(Erase heading not required.)

Army Form C. 2118

Place	Date	Hour	Summary of Events and Information	Remarks and references to Appendices
O.5.c.7.9.			No damage to our own front, the damage was heavy on our front & CHATEAU WOODS support lines & CHATEAU WOODS in & about times nothing remained as a result of the enemy artillery activity & the night passed quietly. Weather DULL	
"	18/8/17		Day passed uneventfully. A draft of 29 O.R. reported for duty at WOOD CAMP. Casualties O.R. 2 killed 5 wounded Weather DULL	
"	19/8/17		A Wingfeldwebel who stated that he had lost his way, wandered into our lines in the early morning & gave himself up as a prisoner, no information of any importance was obtained from him	

WAR DIARY
INTELLIGENCE SUMMARY

Army Form C. 2118

Place	Date	Hour	Summary of Events and Information	Remarks and references to Appendices
O.S.c.79.	9/8/17		No hostile shelling of any account was reported during the day.	
		8.50 P.M.	Enemy heavily harrassed our line R. of FORRET FARM with a general barrage on & behind FORRET FARM + the OPTIC line afterwards developed into attack but nothing materialised + it is thought that nothing in the way of an attack was intended of this nature.	See MAP "A"
			Weather FAIR Casualties O.R. 5 killed 10 wounded.	
	10/8/17	1.30 am	Four of our posts immediately in front of HOLLEBEKE were advanced about 50 yds for an attack	
		4.35 am	This was the Zero hour which was made by the Division on our left N. of the Canal. The barrage extended over our front, within 5 mins of the commencement of the barrage the enemy retaliated furiously, putting down a very heavy barrage on the HOLLEBEKE — FORRET FARM line. No 123 Brigade on our left sent out several patrols during these operations, which were successful, about 30 prisoners being taken.	
		Dusk	The Battalion was relieved by the 11. R.W. Kents & 1 Coy 12th E.Surreys, relief was carried out successfully to the Battalion proceeded in lorries from the BRASSERIE to MURRUMBIDGEE Camp N.1.a.	
			Casualties O.R. 2 killed 1 wounded Weather FINE	

WAR DIARY
or
INTELLIGENCE SUMMARY

Army Form C. 2118

Place	Date	Hour	Summary of Events and Information	Remarks and references to Appendices
MURRUMBIDGEE CAMP N.S.W.	11/8/17		Battalion spent the day cleaning up in general. Weather SHOWERY. Casualties O.R. 1 wounded	
	12/8/17		Battalion paraded for inspection by the C.O. who expressed his congratulations & thanks to Officers, NCO's & men on their excellent work during the last tour in the trenches, also to the Q.M.S.'s & Transport who had done all that was humanly possible in maintaining the supply of rations etc. to said that he had received congratulations on the Battalion's work from Brigade, Division & Corps Commanders & could not adequately express his pride in being in command of the Battalion whose fame was spreading throughout the whole army in France. The United Methodist attended Church Parade during the morning. Weather FAIR	

WAR DIARY or INTELLIGENCE SUMMARY

Army Form C. 2118

Place	Date	Hour	Summary of Events and Information	Remarks and references to Appendices
MURRUMBIDGEE CAMP	13/8/17		The Companies went for a short route march & had some gas drill. Weather UNSETTLED	
FLÊTRE 27/N.6. HQ. x 2d. 04	14/8/17		Battalion marched to HALLABAST CORNER & were met by 'busses which conveyed them to FLÊTRE where we alighted & marched to camp. H.Q. being in the farm at 27/x.2.c.95.40. The Companies in the surrounding farms & fields. Weather generally fine, occasional thunder showers	
"	15/8/17		Battalion spent the day in Physical & Specialist Training. Weather fine	
"	16/8/17		Battalion was inspected by the Brigadier who expressed his congratulations & thanks to the Batt. for their excellent work during the last tour in the line. The rest of the day was spent in re-organisation of Companies & Specialist training. Weather FINE	
			Reinforcements Lt H.F. WADHAM & 8 O.R. reported for duty.	

Place	Date	Hour	Summary of Events and Information	Remarks and references to Appendices
FLETRE 27/x.2.d.0.4.	17/8/17		The 122nd Inf. Brigade was inspected by Lieut General Sir T.L.N. MORLAND KCB, KCMG, D.S.O. the xth corps commander + Maj General S.T.B. LAWFORD commanding 41st division, both of whom expressed their thanks + congratulations to the Brigade on their recent good work. weather FAIR	
	18/8/17		The Brigade paraded for inspection by the 2nd Army Commander General Sir Herbert C.O. Plumer. G.C.M.G. G.C.V.O. K.C.B A.D.C. During the day Companies paraded for Baths, + Snipers fent for practice on tzyange During the night hostile aircraft bombed an area toward some casualties to other units in its Division. weather Unsettled	
	19/8/17		Battalion attended Church Parade + afterwards Companies went for a short root march. Draft Lt S GREENLESS, Lt R.H. MONTAGUE + 78 OR reported for duty weather FINE	

WAR DIARY
or
INTELLIGENCE SUMMARY
(Erase heading not required.)

Army Form C. 2118

Page 11.

Place	Date	Hour	Summary of Events and Information	Remarks and references to Appendices
STAPLE	20/8/17		Battalion marched to the STAPLE - EBBLINGHAM area. Weather Fine	
ACQUIN 27A/V.22.a	21/8/17		The Battalion marched to LE NIEPPE where they were met by lorries which conveyed 500 of them to ACQUIN, the 'buses returned & picked up the remainder on the road. The Battalion billeted in the village HQ at V.22.a.7.9 Weather FINE	
"	22/8/17		Battalion spent the day in the training of Specialists. a draft of 23 O.R. reported for duty. Weather FINE	
"	23/8/17		Specialist training during the morning. 3 Officers + 23 O.R. proceeded by 'bus to WIMEREUX for a days outing Weather SHOWRY	

Army Form C. 2118

WAR DIARY
or
INTELLIGENCE SUMMARY
(Erase heading not required.)

Page 12.

Place	Date	Hour	Summary of Events and Information	Remarks and references to Appendices
ACQUIN	24/8/17		The 41st Division Paraded for inspection by Field Marshal Sir Douglas Haig. K.T. G.C.V.O. K.C.I.E. Unfortunately a sharp shower started when Sir D. Haig arrived & lasted until after the inspection. weather SHOWRY	
"	25/8/17		Battalion spent the day in the training of specialists. weather FAIR	
"	26/8/17		Battalion attended Church Parade. 3 Officers + 22 OR went by lorry to BOULOGNE for a day outing. weather FAIR	
"	27/8/17		Battalion spent the day in Specialist + General Training. Officers also attended Kueing School. weather RAIN	

WAR DIARY or INTELLIGENCE SUMMARY

Army Form C. 2118

Page 13.

Place	Date	Hour	Summary of Events and Information	Remarks and references to Appendices
ACQUIN	28/8/17		Officers Riding School, Specialist & General Training. Weather RAIN	
"	29/8/17		The day was spent chiefly in lectures in billets owing to the rain. A draft of 15 OR reported for duty. Weather RAIN	
"	30/8/17		Officers attended Riding School, B.C. & Stop went firing on ranges. Major C. MURDOCH from the 11th R.W. Kents reported for duty. Weather FAIR	
"	31/8/17		Training in Assault Tactics. Capt MACLACHAN RAMC reported for duty vice Capt DAVIES returned to 140th F.A. Weather SHOWERY	
			140 were admitted to Hospital during the month from civilian (50 of these went away with Trench Feet from the 1st to the 6th inst).	

Iain Darroad
LIEUT.-COL. CMDG.
15 HAMPSHIRE REGT.

1. I am at................................ and am consolidating.
   .... and have consolidated.

2. I am held up by M.G. at................................

3. I need :— Ammunition.   Water and rations.
             Bombs.   Very lights.
             Rifle Bombs.   Stokes shells.

4. Counter attack forming up at................................

5. I am in touch with................................ on Right at................................
                                                       Left

6. I am not in touch on Right
                       Left

7. Am being shelled from................................

8. Present strength............ rifles. Reinforcements required:—
   .... Platoons.   .... Sections rifle bombers.
   .... Sections riflemen.   ....   ”   Lewis gunners.
   ....   ”   bombers.

9. Hostile .... { Battery / Machine Gun / Trench Mortar } active at................................

Time................ m.   Name................................

Date................   Platoon................................

                                 Company................................

                                 Battalion................................

Army Form C. 2118.

HANTS

15 Hants Rgt

122/41

Vol 17

9 photos

M.R.

WAR DIARY
or
INTELLIGENCE SUMMARY
(Erase heading not required.)

Page 1.

Place	Date	Hour	Summary of Events and Information	Remarks and references to Appendices
ACQUIN 27A/V.22.a.	1/9/17		Battalion spent the day in the training of Specialists	
"	2/9/17		Battalion attended Church Parade. The C.O. presented Divisional cards to the following Officer N.C.O.'s + men :— 2/Lt S. LASENBY. 8024. A/C.S.M. F.COLLIS. 8018 Sgt. G. WARREN 11775 Sgt. E. CROSS 23138 A/Cpl. F. SCOTT. 15557. Pte. J. WHATELEY. 380176 Pte W. GILBERT 26075 L/Sgt. C. NORTH 10836 L/Cpl. P. COOMBES 10256. - R.H. PARSONS 20737 - C. WINGATE 26071 " S. FAULKNER 26946 " R.H. DAVEY 23477 - W.V. MINNETT, 18004 - T.G. SMITH.	
"	3/9/17		Battalion spent the day in the training of Specialists	
"	4/9/17		General Training	
"	5/9/17		Practice in assault tactics. The following officers reported for duty 2/Lt F H J DAMP (A Co) 2/Lt G.M. MEATYARD (B Coy) 2/Lt L.B RAYNBIRD (C Coy)	
"	6/9/17		Battalion carried out a demonstration attack	

Army Form C. 2118.

WAR DIARY
or
INTELLIGENCE SUMMARY
(Erase heading not required.)

Instructions regarding War Diaries and Intelligence Summaries are contained in F. S. Regs., Part II. and the Staff Manual respectively. Title Pages will be prepared in manuscript.

Place	Date	Hour	Summary of Events and Information	Remarks and references to Appendices
ACQUIN 27A/N.22.a	7/9/17		Specialist Training during morning. The Battalion Sports were started in the afternoon + continued on the 9th inst. Four OR reported for duty	
"	8/9/17		Battalion attended a Gas demonstration by the Divisional Gas Officer at MORNINGTIEM WINDMILL. 2/Lt H.W.GREEN reported for duty (B Coy)	
"	9/9/17		Battalion attended Church Parade, after which Brigadier General F.W.TOWSEY presented medal ribands to the undermentioned Officer N.CO's + men. A/Capt. C. C. OXBORROW 8208 Sgt G. WARREN 11776 " E. CROSS 26975 L/Sgt C. NORTH 26971 L/Sgt S.FAULKNER 25158 A/Cpl F SCOTT 10836 L/Cpl P. COOMBES 19256 Pte R.H.PARSONS 20615 - W.J. LAKE 15557 - J. WHATLEY 20737 Pte C WINGATE 12847 - F WATERS M.G.S.M. F. COLLIS (BAR G.M. MD) The Battalion Sports were continued for the 9th inst. at 11.0 A.M. for the rest of the day t WEATHER FINE	
	10/9/17		Battalion practiced the new form of attack in depth Weather FINE	
	11/9/17		Specialist Training + Baths. 10 OR reported for duty Weather FINE	

WAR DIARY or INTELLIGENCE SUMMARY

Army Form C. 2118.

Place	Date	Hour	Summary of Events and Information	Remarks and references to Appendices
ACQUIN 27F/V.22.a.	12/9/17		The 122 INF BGE practiced the attack for the forthcoming operations. weather FAIR	
"	13/9/17		Specialist Training. weather FAIR	
WALLON-CAPPEL 27/N.35.b	14/9/17		Battalion commenced the march back to the line, by route TATINGHEM – ARQUES – LE NIEPPE – WALLON-CAPPEL covering 18 miles in full marching order	
LE ROUCKLOOSHILLE	15/9/17		Battalion continued the march — WALLON-CAPPEL — HONDEGHEM STATION — CAESTRE – FLETRE – LE ROUCKLOOSHILLE. weather FINE	
RIDGE-WOOD	16/9/17		Battalion continued the march – LE ROUCKLOOSHILLE — WESTOUTRE — LA CLYTTE — MILLABAST CORNER — RIDGE WOOD	
"	17/9/17		Battalion spent the morning organising & equipping men for the line, the afternoon was spent in rest.	
HEDGE STREET TUNNELS 28/I.30.6.a.7.			Battalion left RIDGE WOOD.. 500 strong + relieved the 9th Yorks + Lancs (39th Division) in the line E. of BODMIN COPSE, H.Q. at 1.30.6.a.7. Details marched back to CARNARVON CAMP (M.1D.6.8.9). 13. O.R. reported for duty. weather FINE	

Army Form C. 2118.

WAR DIARY
or
INTELLIGENCE SUMMARY
(Erase heading not required.)

Instructions regarding War Diaries and Intelligence Summaries are contained in F. S. Regs., Part II. and the Staff Manual respectively. Title Pages will be prepared in manuscript.

Place	Date	Hour	Summary of Events and Information	Remarks and references to Appendices
HEDGE STREET TUNNELS	18/9/17		There was lively artillery activity on both sides, otherwise day passed uneventfully. A draft of 3 O.R. reported to Details Camp for duty. weather SHOWERY	
" "	19/9/17		Artillery activity continues. A draft of 6 O.R. reported to Details Camp for duty. During the night the Battalion took up its position for the attack, all arrangements being carried out smoothly & uneventfully. weather FAIR during day RAIN all night	
	20/9/17	5.40 A.M.	was Zero hour for an attack which was made by the 122nd Inf Brigade with TOWER TRENCH East of GHELUVELT as its final objective. The attack was made on a two Battalion front, each Batt on a two Company front & was organised in depth. The Order of Battle was :— 15th Batt HANTS REGT on the left, 18th K.R.R.C. on the right, who were allotted the task of taking the first remand objectives	

WAR DIARY
or
INTELLIGENCE SUMMARY
(Erase heading not required.)

Army Form C. 2118

Place	Date	Hour	Summary of Events and Information	Remarks and references to Appendices
			The RED and BLUE Line (west task of BASSEVILLEBERS respectively) after which the 11th WEST KENTS. on the left and 12th E SURREYS on the right were to pass through and assault the final objective the GREEN LINE (TOWER TRENCH).	
			The assembly took place without great difficulty and the attack was launched at 5.10AM.	
			The 15 tanks were checked by a strong point which had been untouched by the barrage about 6 minutes after the start, which was soon overcome by the gallantry of Officers and men in storming the position. After the BLUE line which the 15 task objective was reached without difficulty. Casualties were heavy including all four Company Commanders. A the counter attack was threatened from N.E (on the MENIN ROAD) was dispersed by rifle & machine gun fire. The 11th WEST KENTS passed through so but failed to take their objective owing to strong resistance from the neighbourhood of TOWER HAMLETS. and fell back on to the BLUE LINE	
		5.30	at 5.30 Orders were received to the effect that two Battalions of 109nd Infantry Brigade (the 15 Hants + 11th WEST KENTS—) were to attack the GREEN LINE. The 11th WEST KENTS were too disorganized at the time so that the attack was carried out by 130 men of the 15th HANTS.	
			The position was captured and over 40 prisoners, a Battalion Commander and	

WAR DIARY
or
INTELLIGENCE SUMMARY
(Erase heading not required.)

Army Form C. 2118

Place	Date	Hour	Summary of Events and Information	Remarks and references to Appendices
	2/9/17	10 AM	his adjutant, two machine guns and one field gun were taken. The objective was consolidated and held against several counter attacks in spite of the fact that the 123rd Brigade who attacked on our right, failed to reach their objective.	
			At about 10 AM 2/Lt M.S. Moore who was in comm and of the GREEN LINE slightly withdrew his men to avoid our own barrage, which was being fired at GREEN LINE through false information. After this, he returned to his position - Green line.	
		3.35 pm	Battalion observers reported enemy massing for counter attacks in the valley S.E. and the S.O.S. was sent up. The enemy, however, were repulsed by rifle and Machine Gun fire before our own Artillery had opened liquid fire contained were seen on the backs of some of the enemy, one of which was seen to burst into flames.	
		3.45 pm & 6.30 pm	The GREEN LINE was then barraged by the enemy and again shortly afterwards heavily bombarded by our own Artillery who thought the position abandoned	
			WEATHER FINE	

Army Form C. 2118.

WAR DIARY
or
INTELLIGENCE SUMMARY
(Erase heading not required.)

Place	Date	Hour	Summary of Events and Information	Remarks and references to Appendices
	22/9/17	4·0 A.M.	The Coys put a practice barrage in front of GREEN LINE + at 8·30 AM	
		8·30 AM	2/Lt M.S. MOORE turned up with the remnants of his garrison. He had taken his party forward again after the shelling on the morning of the 21st inst to his former outpost, caught by both our own and the enemy's barrage, he had about 10 men (although they had lost their rifles & rations in however, the barrage) armed themselves with 3 German rifles, ammunition + 3 German grenades each, + prepared to meet any attack. They remained in their forward positions until 7·0 AM on the 22nd inst: when they returned to our lines, bringing behind an anti-tank gun + 2 MG's they had captured but were unable to bring back.	
		11·0 P.M.	With the exception of heavy shelling the remainder of the day was uneventful until about 11·0 PM when the Battalion was relieved by the 3rd Division + proceeded to camp at RIDGE WOOD.	

The Battalion suffered the following casualties during the operation:

```
                                6 officers killed
                                7     "     wounded
                               ___
                                13

                               49 o.R. killed
                                3  -    Missing believed killed
                              248  -    wounded
                              ___
                              300
```

5 o.R. not yet reported
31 o.R. missing
___
36

TOTAL 349

WAR DIARY or INTELLIGENCE SUMMARY

Army Form C. 2118.

Place	Date	Hour	Summary of Events and Information	Remarks and references to Appendices
CAESTRE	23/9/17	9.0 AM	Batt'n marched from CARNARVON CAMP to OUDERDOM & entrained for CAESTRE	
		6.0 PM	" " " " RIDGE WOOD " "	weather FINE
"	24/9/17		Battalion spent the day in rest & cleaning up. The C.O. thanked & congratulated all ranks on their excellent work during recent operations. 82 O.R. reported for duty.	
			A draft of 12 Officers and 307 O.R. from the 1/1st HAMPSHIRE CARABINIERS YEOMANRY reported for duty	weather FINE
	25/9/17			
	26/9/17		Battalion went for a short route march after which the draft of CARABINIERS were inspected by BRIGADIER GEN'L TOWSEY	weather FINE
TETEGHEM	27/9/17		Battalion moved to the TETEGHEM AREA	
K/22.				weather FINE
BRAY DUNES	28/9/17		Battalion marched to BRAY DUNES & pitched camp just outside the village among the DUNES	weather FINE

WAR DIARY or INTELLIGENCE SUMMARY

Army Form C. 2118.

Place	Date	Hour	Summary of Events and Information	Remarks and references to Appendices
BRAY DUNES	29/9/17		Companies went for a short route march + went on bathing parades	

TOTAL CASUALTIES OF THE BATTALION
May 2nd 1916 – Oct 1st 1917.

Officers:—

	Killed	Wounded	Pris. of War
1916 Sep 15	6	3	
Oct 7th	3	2	
1917 June 7	2	6	
July 23 – Aug 11	1	5	
Sep 17-22	6	6	1
Other Dates	6	17	
	24	39	1

Other Ranks:—

	Killed	Wounded	Pris. of War or Missing
Sep 15 '16	41	197	56
Oct 7	36	157	16
June 7	38	135	3
July 23 – Aug 11	31	103	7
Sep 17-22	49	248	34
Other Dates	48	261	1 + 5
	243	1081	117 5

Total – Officers 64
Men 1446
1510

HONOURS & AWARDS – May 2nd 1916 – Oct 1st 1917

Bar to D.S.O.	1
M.C.	13
D.C.M.	4
M.M.	60
Bar to M.M.	2
Mention	7
Foreign Orders	2
	99

Army Form C. 2118.

WAR DIARY
or
INTELLIGENCE SUMMARY

(Erase heading not required.)

15 Hampshire Vol 18

Instructions regarding War Diaries and Intelligence Summaries are contained in F.S. Regs., Part II. and the Staff Manual respectively. Title Pages will be prepared in manuscript.

Place	Date	Hour	Summary of Events and Information	Remarks and references to Appendices
BRAY DUNES 19/D.2.c	1/10/17		Battalion spent the day in General & Specialist Training.	
"	2/10/17		General & Specialist Training. 2/Lt C.C. NEWMAN and 6 O.R. reported for duty	
"	3/10/17		General & Specialist Training. 2 O.R. reported for duty	
"	4/10/17		" " " 1 O.R " "	
"	5/10/17	10.A.M	Major General LAWFORD inspected the Battalion on the beach, after which the Battalion proceeded with General Training	
"	6/10/17		General & Specialist Training. 2/Lt E.M. TREVETT & 2/Lt R.F. REYNOLDS reported for duty.	
"	7/10/17		At 1.A.M. we adopted Winter Time. Battalion attended Church Parade.	
"	8/10/17		A draft of 119 O.R. from the 1/1st HAMPSHIRE CARABINIERS YEOMANRY reported for duty. Major C.G. MURDOCH assumes command of the Battalion	

Army Form C. 2118.

WAR DIARY
or
INTELLIGENCE SUMMARY
(Erase heading not required.)

2.

Instructions regarding War Diaries and Intelligence Summaries are contained in F. S. Regs., Part II. and the Staff Manual respectively. Title Pages will be prepared in manuscript.

Place	Date	Hour	Summary of Events and Information	Remarks and references to Appendices
BRAY DUNES 19/D.2.c	9/10/17		The draft of CARABINIERS which reported yesterday were inspected by the C.O.	
"	10/10/17		The day was spent in RE-ORGANISATION	
"	11/10/17		General & Specialist Training	
"	12/10/17		" "	
"	13/10/17		" "	
"	14/10/17		Battalion attended Church Parade, after which, Brigadier General TOWSEY presented Divisional Cards to 19 O.R.	
WILTSHIRE CAMP (COXYDE BAINS) 11/X.1.6.5.8.	15/10/17		Battalion marched from BRAY DUNES to COXYDE BAINS and relieved the 32nd ROYAL FUSILIERS at WILTSHIRE CAMP	
"	16/10/17		Battalion spent the day in General & Specialist Training	
"	17/10/17		A & B Coys furnished working parties of 1 Officer + 75 O.R. each 2/Lt J.G. GEERING + 2/Lt A.F. McKIE reported for duty	

Army Form C. 2118.

WAR DIARY
or
INTELLIGENCE SUMMARY

(Erase heading not required.)

Instructions regarding War Diaries and Intelligence Summaries are contained in F. S. Regs., Part II. and the Staff Manual respectively. Title Pages will be prepared in manuscript.

3.

Place	Date	Hour	Summary of Events and Information	Remarks and references to Appendices
WILTSHIRE CAMP 11/x.1.6.5.8	18/10/17		C + D Coys supplied Working Parties of 1 Officer + 75 O.R. each, remainder did General Training. 9 O.R. reported for duty	
"	19/10/17		A + B Coys supplied Working Parties of 1 Officer + 75 O.R. each "	
"	20/10/17		C + D " " " "	
		6.0 PM	Officers + N.C.O's attended lecture by M.O. on Trench Feet	
"	21/10/17		A + B Coys supplied Working Parties of 1 Officer + 75 O.R. each, remainder attended Church Parade	
"	22/10/17		C + D Coys supplied Working Parties of 1 Officer + 75 O.R. each, remainder on General Training	
"	23/10/17		A + B Coys " " " " 1 Officer + 75 O.R. each "	
			65 O.R. reported for duty	
"	24/10/17		C + D Coys supplied Working Parties of 1 Officer + 75 O.R. each "	

Army Form C. 2118.

WAR DIARY
or
INTELLIGENCE SUMMARY
(Erase heading not required.)

Instructions regarding War Diaries and Intelligence Summaries are contained in F.S. Regs., Part II. and the Staff Manual respectively. Title Pages will be prepared in manuscript.

Place	Date	Hour	Summary of Events and Information	Remarks and references to Appendices
WILTSHIRE CAMP 11/x.1.b.5.8	25/10/17		A+B Coys supplied working parties of 1 Officer + 75 O.R. each, remainder General Training	
"	26/10/17		C + D " " " " " " "	
"	27/10/17		A+B " " " " " " "	
"	28/10/17		Casualties 2 O.R. wounded	
"			Working Parties had 17 O.R. casualties all wounded. Batt attended Church Parade	
St POL SUR MER 19/H.2.d.65.95	29/10/17		Battalion were relieved at WILTSHIRE CAMP by the 3rd South African L.I. (9th Division) + marched to COXYDE BAINS where they embussed + proceeded to SAINT POL sur MER + were billeted in the Town. H.Q. being at H.2.d.65.95	
"	30/10/17		Battalion spent the day in Kit inspections + in repairing surplus kit to a minimum. 2nd Lt/ F.H. HARRISON + 31 O.R. joined for duty	
"	31/10/17		Battalion went for a route march. 36 O.R. returned to duty from R.E.'s	

www.ingramcontent.com/pod-product-compliance
Lightning Source LLC
Chambersburg PA
CBHW081542160426
43191CB00011B/1820